PRAYERS FOR THE CHURCH YEAR

TRACES
OF GLORY

PRAYERS FOR THE CHURCH YEAR

TRACES OF GLORY

DAVID ADAM

MOREHOUSE PUBLISHING
HARRISBURG, PENNSYLVANIA

First published in Great Britain 1999
SPCK

Morehouse Publishing
P.O. Box 1321
Harrisburg, PA 17105

Morehouse Publishing is a division of The Morehouse Group.

Printed in Great Britain

Cover design by Trude Brummer

Library of Congress Cataloging-in-Publication Data
Adam, David.
    Traces of glory : prayers for the church year, Year B / David Adam.
    p. cm.
  ISBN 0-8192-1824-3 (pbk.)
  1. Common lectionary. 2. Church year—Prayer-books and devotions—
English. 3. Anglican Communion—Prayer-books and devotions—English.
I. Title.
  BX5147.L4 A33 1999
  264'.036—dc21

99 - 19746
CIP

Contents

In memory of
Will Taylor, 1942–1998
In his life, he showed many traces of glory

Introduction

I enjoy watching a good detective story, it fascinates me to see how far forensic science can go. I am told that wherever you visit you take traces of that place away with you. Wherever you go little pieces of that place cling to you. If you visit a certain house some of the atmosphere of that house becomes part of you. If you have physical contact with another person something rubs off. If you dance with someone wearing perfume a little of it attaches itself to you. The company you keep shows in your life, for good or for bad. It was said of the disciples that 'they had been with Jesus'. There was something in their attitude, something in their reactions that said they had been with Jesus and people noticed.

When Moses went into the tent of meeting, the cloud came down; when he came out of the Tent of Meeting his face shone, his face shone for he had been with God. I know many shining people who are radiant with the love and light of the Lord. I can tell that some of the people I meet have been with Jesus, by their reactions to what life brings before them. There is no doubt that if we spend time with God it shows, and if we do not spend time with God that shows also. There are some people you can say of, 'they are friendly with God'.

Places also have traces of glory. High up on the North Yorks Moors looking towards Roseberry Topping there is a pond. Many a day the pond reflects the sunlight and looks bright when its surroundings are dark. The cover of this book shows this pond reflecting traces of glory. But it is glorious for another reason; here around this pond, when he was a boy, James Cook used to sail his little boats. Later in life he would circumnavigate the world. Here away from the sea he expressed love for boats. More than one person has said to me, 'Captain Cook used to sail little boats on this pond.' The famous captain has left a little of his glory here.

The island I live on was the home of many saints. Aidan came here and founded a monastery, Chad, Cedd, Wilfrid, Cuthbert all spent times of prayer and dedication on this island. Here Eadfrith wrote the Lindisfarne Gospels to the glory of God and St Cuthbert. Later the Benedictines built a daughter house to their monastery in Durham. All have left traces of themselves and their work. They not only transformed this little island, they transformed England. Most of what they achieved was possible because of the time they spent with their God. There was no doubt in their minds that God is the priority. They would well understand St Augustine who said: 'Lord to turn away from you is to fall; to turn to you is to rise. To stand before you is to abide forever.' If life is to have traces eternal it must have the Eternal with it and around it. Now in this world we need to show traces of glory. I believe that sharing in the intercession of our Lord, in praying regularly for others, traces of the love and presence of our God are revealed through us and within us.

Intercession, such as in this book, is not a pleading with God but rather a uniting with him; it is not about manipulating the Almighty but rather co-operating with him. Prayer does not call God down, for he is already among us, but it does transform our awareness. All intercession needs to begin with an opening of our lives to our God. Before any words we should spend as much time as possible resting in and rejoicing in the presence. It is then far easier to see the people we pray for as surrounded by the love and the power of God. This is why the Communion Service has us hear the Scriptures and be in silence before we speak of our needs and the needs of the world. We need to discover traces of glory in our everyday lives, and this is very possible if we are willing to spend time with our God.

For the prayers of the church to be enriched, it demands a praying people. I believe that the best preparation for Sunday worship is to use the readings for the coming Sunday throughout the week as an inspiration for prayer and intercession. If you add to this the reading of a daily newspaper or the watching of the news, the one should influence and transform the other. Take the reading for the coming Sunday and if possible read it aloud; say the words and let them resonate in your hearing. Pick out the pieces that have extra meaning, that seem to speak to you, and repeat them a few times each day. Let the words sink into your mind: let them transform your thinking. Relate what you have read to the world around you, bring your experience to bear on your Bible reading. Use your mind, and fill your mind with these good things: from the mouth to the mind and then to the heart. Let what you read stir your affections, let it move your emotions. Learn that God in love moves towards you, for you are in the heart of God. Let God enter fully into your heart. Invite your God into the very centre of your being. From the mouth to the mind to the heart: now let it work, bring your will into action. Allow yourself to re-act to the word of God, let it move in and out of your hopes and fears, your concerns and plans. Let all be tinged with traces of glory. In our words, our thoughts, our affections and our deeds let there be traces of God's presence, for as always 'The Lord is here'.

How much richer our Sunday worship would be if we prepared ourselves in this way. If we do not pray daily throughout the week, we should not expect to find prayer easy or fulfilling on Sundays. What we do in church must be a reflection of our daily living. This book is to help you to build up good habits and good practices. I hope that it will bring you to see the traces of glory in the world about you, in your home and in your life. It is written so that you can use these prayers at home and so enrich the prayer life of your church. I hope you use this book as a launching pad for your own ideas and prayers.

The layout of the book corresponds with the second year, Year B, of the Common Worship Lectionary as adopted by the

Church of England, the Scottish Episcopal Church, the Church in Wales and other churches within the Anglican Communion. This is very close to the Common Lectionary of the Roman Catholic Church and is used by other denominations. The Lectionary is designed as a three-year cycle and this book is designed for the second year, designated as Year B. For every week of the year, I have provided an extra prayer for the week, a list of intercessions, an offering of peace and a blessing. With the readings for the Sunday, each week could form the basis of family worship, or worship for a group, as well as the single individual. The intercessions follow the pattern as in many books of prayer: we pray for the church, the world, our loved ones, the ill and the needy, and we remember the saints and loved ones departed. If we are willing quietly to use this book, centring our thoughts and words in the presence of God, it will transform us and our outlook. Use this book to discover traces of glory not only in the world and the church but in your loved ones and in yourselves.

Advent

The First Sunday of Advent

Isaiah 64. 1–9 : Ps 80. 1–7 [17–19] : 1 Corinthians 1. 3–9 : Mark 13. 24–37

Come, Lord, come down, come in, come among us.
Enter into our darkness with your light.
Come fill our emptiness with your presence.
Dispel the clouds and reveal your glory.
Come refresh, renew, restore us.
Come Lord, come down, come in, come among us. **Amen.**

Come, Lord, be known in your church,
for without you we have no message, we have no power.
Come fill us with your presence,
that we may proclaim your peace.
Lord, make us aware, alert to your coming,
that we may reveal your glory in all the world.
We pray for those that walk in darkness,
that they may see your light.
We remember those whose lives are clouded with troubles
and pray that they may behold your glory.
Lord, stir up your strength
and come among us.

Come, Lord, and give peace to your world.
Disperse the clouds of war and violence, of calamity and
    disaster.
Let your power and your glory be revealed to the nations.
We pray for all who watch and wait while we sleep:
for the police, hospital workers and ambulance workers,
for fire fighters, and for all who work in the dark hours of the
    night.
Lord, stir up your strength
and come among us.

Come, Lord, be known in our homes,
that our homes may reflect your love.
Come in our work places that they may reflect your glory;
that we may rejoice in each other's presence,
that we may be fully aware of others and sensitive to their
    needs.
Lord, stir up your strength
and come among us.

Come, Lord, to all who are unable to cope at this time;
to all who are weighed down with troubles.
We pray for the ill and for those who have the care of them.
We remember those whose lives are clouded with despair.
We pray for the depressed and the suicidal.
We remember friends and loved ones in their
    troubles ....
Lord, stir up your strength
and come among us.

Come, Lord of our salvation, save us and we shall be saved.
We pray for friends and loved ones departed, especially
    for ....
May they now rejoice in the fullness of your presence and your
    glory.
Lord, stir up your strength
and come among us.

THE PEACE

Grace to you and peace from God our Father, and the Lord Jesus Christ.
The peace of the Lord be always with you
and also with you.

THE BLESSING

May the Lord find you alert to his coming, open to his presence, aware of his love; and the blessing of God Almighty, the Father, the Son and the Holy Spirit, be among you, and remain with you always. **Amen.**

The Second Sunday of Advent

———

Isaiah 40. 1–11 : Ps. 85. [1–2] 8–13 : 2 Peter 3. 8–15a : Mark 1. 1–8

Lord, grant us a glimpse of your glory:
open our eyes to your coming to us,
that we may know you are with us always,
and that you are a very present help in trouble.
Lord, as you abide in us, and we abide in you,
may we show traces of your glory in our lives,
and so glorify you, Lord Jesus,
Who lives and reigns with the Father and the Holy Spirit,
one God, now and for ever. **Amen.**

Lord, you come to us in power, to send us out in your Name.
Strengthen us to proclaim the Good News without fear.

7

May we be able to say 'Here is your God',
and show forth your glory in our land.
We pray for preachers of the word and ministers of the
    sacraments;
for all who lead worship, for choirs and organists.
We pray for spiritual leaders and writers, for all who seek to
    witness to your love.
Show us your mercy, O Lord,
and grant us your salvation.

We pray for all who influence the minds of your people:
for the press and for broadcasters,
for those who through the spoken or written word affect the
    way we live.
We pray for teachers and leaders of young people,
for all who make decisions about our future or set us standards
    to follow,
for all who influence our minds and our hearts.
Show us your mercy, O Lord,
and grant us your salvation.

Lord, in our homes let us be wise in our use of words,
that we may dwell in love and peace with each other.
We pray for the gift of good communication.
We remember all who have stopped speaking to each other.
We pray for areas where words are used to hurt,
for homes where there is abuse, and places where there is
    violence and cruelty.
Show us your mercy, O Lord,
and grant us your salvation.

Lord, you restore, you forgive, you bring peace.
We pray for broken peoples, for the broken-hearted and the
    broken-spirited.
We pray for the guilt-ridden, for the disturbed,
for those who are unable to communicate with others,
that they may know your peace and your love.

We remember friends and loved ones with whom we have lost contact through illness.
We pray for all who are ill at this time,
especially ....
Show us your mercy, O Lord,
and grant us your salvation.

As we wait for your coming in glory, we pray for all who have passed into the fullness of your kingdom. We give you thanks for the saints in glory, for our benefactors who have gone before us. We pray for all our loved ones departed from us.
Show us your mercy, O Lord,
and grant us your salvation.

THE PEACE

Dear friends, while you are waiting for the day of God, strive to be found at peace by him.
The peace of the Lord be always with you
and also with you.

THE BLESSING

The Lord comes to you this day in great power:
he comes as a shepherd to care for his flock;
he comes to heal, to restore, to forgive, to bring you home;
he comes to you;
and the blessing...

The Third Sunday of Advent

Isaiah 61. 1–4, 8–11 : Ps. 126 (*or* Magnificat) : 1 Thessalonians 5. 16–24 :
John 1. 6–8, 19–28

Come, Holy Spirit of God, come upon us,
that you may send us out in your power.
Fill us with your grace and goodness,
that we may be able to bring the Good News to the oppressed,
to comfort the broken-hearted,
and to bring liberty and freedom to your people;
through Jesus Christ our Lord,
who lives and reigns with you and the Father,
for ever and ever. **Amen.**

Holy Lord, you come to us, you inspire us, you enable us;
grant that we may proclaim your loving presence
and show your saving power.
Let your church be seen to be working for justice and
    righteousness, for liberty and peace;
Lord, that we may live at peace and oppress no one.
Make us instruments of peace within our communities and
    within our homes.
Lord of freedom,
hear us.

We remember before you all who are seeking freedom:
we pray for nations burdened with great debt,
for families who have lost their homes, peoples denied justice.
We pray for all who are suffering from violence or tyranny.

10

We pray for the work of Amnesty International, we remember
all who care for prisoners.
We pray for any who are hostages at this time,
especially ....
Lord of freedom,
hear us.

Lord, teach us to appreciate what we have and to be aware of
all that is done for us.
Let us not take each other for granted.
Let us hold fast to all that is good and abstain from every form
of evil.
May our homes be homes of holiness and hospitality, of grace
and goodness.
Lord of freedom,
hear us.

We remember in your holy presence, God of liberty,
all whose lives have been diminished by poverty or neglect,
all whose confidence has been lost through harsh treatment or
scorn.
We pray for those who have been betrayed, especially those
betrayed by loved ones.
We remember all who have suffered through robbery or
slander.
We pray for all who have lost their dignity through illness.
We remember friends and loved ones in their troubles,
especially ....
We pray that all who are bereaved at this time may be
strengthened.
Lord of freedom,
hear us.

Lord, you have done great things for us already, and yet, greater
things are to come.
We pray for all who have departed from us,
especially ....

11

May they be numbered with your saints and know the glorious
  liberty of the children of God.
Lord of freedom,
hear us.

THE PEACE

The God of peace sanctify you entirely; may your body, soul
and spirit be kept sound and blameless.
The peace of the Lord be always with you
and also with you.

THE BLESSING

Rejoice in the Lord: pray without ceasing, give thanks in all
circumstances.
Do not quench the Spirit. Hold fast to what is good, abstain
from all evil.
And the blessing...

The Fourth Sunday of Advent

———

2 Samuel 7. 1–11, 16: Magnificat *or* Ps. 89. 1–4, 19–26 (*or* 1–8):
Romans 16. 25–27: Luke 1. 26–38

Lord, you are with us wherever we go:
you are our God and the Rock of our salvation.
You come to us each day and always.
Lord, open our eyes to your presence,

open our hearts to your love,
open our minds to your indwelling;
through Jesus Christ our Lord,
who is alive and reigns with you and the Holy Spirit,
one God, now and for ever. **Amen.**

Lord, we give you thanks for the peace of this place,
the deep and lasting peace you give to us.
We pray for all who go out in mission, for all who proclaim the
   Good News;
we remember house groups, church-planters, and all who build
   up the Body of Christ.
We give thanks for all who, with various talents, seek to
   establish your kingdom.
Lord of all creation,
equip us to serve you.

We pray for all in their various callings,
that they may be sensitive to the needs of others and to the
   world about them.
We remember the unemployed, the recently redundant, and
   those who have never worked.
We pray for all organizations and agencies that care for the
   poor and rejected of our world.
Lord of all creation,
equip us to serve you.

We give thanks that you come to us, in our homes and in our
   work.
We give thanks that we have found favour with you, and that
   you love us.
In our homes, make us attentive to your word and ready to do
   your will.
We pray for expectant mothers, for lone parents, for those
   adopting children.
We remember children in places of danger or violence, those
   being led astray by others.

Lord of all creation,
equip us to serve you.

Lord, you are our strength and salvation:
you alone can make us whole,
you alone give life which is eternal.
We pray for all who are in need at this time:
for those whose lives lack peace, for all who are disturbed.
We pray for the homeless, for the work of Shelter, for the street
    children of our world.
We remember all who are in trouble or in sickness,
    especially ....
We pray for all who are caring for the needs of others.
Lord of all creation,
equip us to serve you.

We give thanks for all who have faithfully served you and are
    now in the fullness of your glory.
We pray for loved ones departed,
    especially ....
Lord of all creation,
equip us to serve you.

THE PEACE

God is able to strengthen you and keep you.
The peace of the Lord be always with you
and also with you.

THE BLESSING

To the only wise God be praise and glory for ever and ever.
To God who is our Rock and our Salvation be blessing and
honour.
And the blessing...

Christmas

Christmas Day

———

Any of these sets of readings may be used on the evening of Christmas Eve and on Christmas Day.

I	II	III
Isaiah 9. 2–7	Isaiah 62. 6–12	Isaiah 52. 7–10
Ps. 96	Ps. 97	Ps. 98
Titus 2. 11–14	Titus 3. 4–7	Hebrews 1. 1–4 [5–12]
Luke 2. 1–14 [15–20]	Luke 2. [1–7] 8–20	John 1. 1–14

Blessing and honour and glory and power be to our God,
for his love revealed in the Word made flesh.
Blessing and honour and glory and power be to our God,
coming among us and sharing our humanity.
Blessing and honour and glory and power be to our God,
filling Mary with the life of the Divine.
Blessing and honour and glory and power be to our God,
for our salvation, for bringing joy and peace into our world;
through Jesus Christ our Lord. **Amen.**

Praise be to God in his great love for us.
He has entered our darkness with his great light.
He comes as our God and yet as a child.
Lord, help us and your whole church to walk as children of the
    light.

Teach us to see your presence in each other:
to be aware that what we do to each other we do to you.
We give thanks for the word spoken by the prophets,
but above all for the Word made flesh dwelling among us.
May your whole church proclaim this Good News with joy.
Lord Jesus, born of the Virgin Mary,
be born in us today.

Glory to God in the highest and on earth peace.
We pray for lasting peace in the Middle East and for Bethlehem
today.
Lord, give peace in the hearts of all, peace in our land, peace
among the nations:
peace in our homes and peace in all our dealings;
peace through him who is the Prince of Peace.
Lord Jesus, born of the Virgin Mary,
be born in us today.

Lord Jesus, born of Mary, you are part of the human family:
you share our joys and our sorrows, our hopes and our fears.
Bless our homes with your loving presence,
be known to be with us, our families and our friends.
Lord Jesus, born of the Virgin Mary,
be born in us today.

Lord Jesus Christ, you came down to lift us up.
You descended that we might ascend.
You became human that we could share in the divine.
We pray for all who are down at this time:
we remember the outcast and the refugee; the homeless peoples
and the street-dwellers.
We pray for the lonely and those who are unloved,
for all who will find this a sad day or a hard day.
Lord Jesus, born of the Virgin Mary,
be born in us today.

We give thanks that you have opened the kingdom of heaven to
all believers.
We pray for loved ones departed from us, that they may be one
with you in your kingdom.
Lord Jesus, born of the Virgin Mary,
be born in us today.

THE PEACE

Glory to God in the highest and on earth peace.
The peace of the Lord be always with you
and also with you.

THE BLESSING

This Holy day, let
the wisdom of the Wonderful Counsellor enlighten you,
the strength of the Mighty God empower you,
the love of the Everlasting Father enfold you,
the peace of the Prince of Peace be about you;
and the blessing...

The First Sunday of Christmas

Isaiah 61.10—62.3 : Ps. 148. [1–6] 7–14 : Galatians 4. 4–7 : Luke 2. 15–21

Lord, give joy to the world:
joy in our hearts, joy in our homes.
Let the joy of God be known among us.

For your love revealed in your manger birth,
we join with the shepherds to glorify and praise you;
through him who came to live among us, Jesus Christ our Lord,
who lives with you and the Holy Spirit,
one God now and for ever. **Amen.**

Lord, we greatly rejoice in your presence among us.
We come to bow with the shepherds,
to kneel with the wise men,
to adore with Joseph,
to hold you in our hearts with Mary.
Let your church proclaim your glory and your love.
We pray for pastors and shepherds of your flock:
for all who go out in mission, for all involved in outreach.
May we reveal you as the Light to lighten all peoples.
Light who lightens all,
shine in our lives.

Lord, we remember with sadness the divisions of our world:
a world not at peace, where people are misused and often
    scorned.
We remember the places of war and violence,
    especially ....
Lord, may the nations come to know that peace which only you
    can give;
we pray that we learn to live together in harmony and
    fellowship.
Light who lightens all,
shine in our lives.

Lord, we give thanks for family life,
for our homes and for those who have cared for us.
We pray for children that are not wanted or who are denied
    love:
for all children taken into care,
for the abandoned, the abused, the ill-treated.
We pray for all who have cared for us ....

Light who lightens all,
shine in our lives.

Lord, we remember all who are lonely this Christmas time:
all who are troubled or sad,
all who are unable to enter into the fullness of joy through
  sickness or bereavement.
We pray for parents anxious about their children.
We remember all who are in the shadow of the fear of death.
We pray today for ....
Light who lightens all,
shine in our lives.

Lord, we remember all who have entered into joy and peace in
  the glory of your kingdom.
We pray especially today for ....
May they rejoice in your presence and your love.
Light who lightens all,
shine in our lives.

THE PEACE

The Lord has caused righteousness and peace to spring up in the
  earth.
The peace of the Lord be always with you
and also with you.

THE BLESSING

The peace of the Prince of Peace,
the love of the Lord of Light,
the joy of Jesus our Saviour,
be within you and about you.
The glory, grace and goodness of God go with you;
and the blessing ...

19

The Second Sunday of Christmas

Jeremiah 31. 7–14 : Ps. 147. 12–20 : Or: Ecclus. 24. 1–12 : *Canticle*: Wisdom of
Solomon 10. 15–21 : Ephesians 1. 3–14 : John 1. [1–9] 10–18

Blessed be you, O God and Father of our Lord Jesus Christ; you
have blessed us with every spiritual blessing in Christ our Lord.
God of love, you have come among us, to renew us, refresh us
and restore us. In you we are ransomed, redeemed, forgiven.
Keep us ever aware of your love and the radiance of your
goodness; through Christ who descended to lift us up and who
lives and reigns with you and the Holy Spirit, one God, now
and for ever. **Amen.**

Lord, that the church may proclaim the joy of the Gospel:
that it may bring your strength and hope to all in need;
that it may reveal your glory in our midst;
Lord, give to your faithful people wisdom and gentleness in all
    their dealings.
We pray today for lay preachers and evangelists,
for teachers in Sunday schools and in Bible study groups.
O Lord Christ, our Redeemer,
save your people who call upon you.

Lord, you are the beginning and the source of all things,
teach us to have respect towards your creation.
We pray for all who are involved in the caring for our planet:
for ecologists, conservationists, for farmers and for fishermen,
for all who seek to supply us with our needs.

O Lord Christ, our Redeemer,
save your people who call upon you.

Eternal light, shine in our hearts,
Deliver us and our loved ones from all evil.
Be known in our homes, that we may be seen to be your people.
We pray for homes where there is strife and division,
where there is a lack of love or a lack of trust;
for all who have been deserted by a loved one.
O Lord Christ, our Redeemer,
save your people who call upon you.

Eternal goodness, deliver your people from all evil.
Guide and direct all who have gone astray.
We pray for all involved with drugs or vice,
for all who walk in darkness, the doubting and despairing,
that all may come to behold your glory and know that they are
    loved.
We pray especially today for ....
O Lord Christ, our Redeemer,
save your people who call upon you.

Eternal God, you are the giver of life which is eternal,
you will not let your loved ones be lost or destroyed.
We pray for our friends and loved ones who are now in your
    kingdom.
O Lord Christ, our Redeemer,
save your people who call upon you.

THE PEACE

The true light that enlightens everyone is come into the world:
the Word is made flesh and now dwells among us.
The peace of the Lord be always with you
and also with you.

THE BLESSING

The Eternal Light shine in your hearts.
The Eternal Goodness deliver you from evil.
The Eternal God grant you a glimpse of glory.
And the blessing...

The Epiphany

The Epiphany

Isaiah 60. 1–6 : Ps. 72. [1–9] 10–15 : Ephesians 3. 1–12 : Matthew 2. 1–12

O Holy Father, who gave guidance to the wise men until they
bowed in worship before our Saviour, lead us to an awareness
of your presence and to bow in adoration before Christ our
Lord, who is alive and reigns with you and the Holy Spirit, one
God, now and for ever. **Amen.**

Great and wonderful God, we seek you.
We look for you. We long for you.
We come and offer our lives, our love, our hopes to you.
God, richer than all we have to offer, we offer you our worship.
We give thanks for the offering of frankincense and pray for all
    who give their lives in adoration.
We pray for the congregation and church to which we belong.
We pray for all leaders of worship, for all who bow in quiet
    adoration.
By the light of your presence,
fill us with your glory.

O God, Creator of all things, we offer you all we have received.
We offer our talents, our possessions, ourselves in your service.
We give you thanks for the gift of gold.

We pray for all who work in commerce: for bankers, for dealers in gold, for gold miners, for ministers of finance.

We remember before you the world's poor, the bankrupt, the underprivileged, the starving.

May all who have received of your bounty share generously with those in need.

By the light of your presence,
fill us with your glory.

O God, whose Son was born into an earthly family, bless our homes and our loved ones.

Reveal your presence in our homes and in our relationships.

We pray for all who are born into sordid homes or into homelessness.

We pray for children who suffer from violence or through neglect.

By the light of your presence,
fill us with your glory.

O God, you share in our sorrows, you enter into our darkness.

You, Lord, come to redeem, release and restore us.

We give thanks for the strange gift of myrrh.

We pray for all who are in pain or in distress, all who are troubled or anxious.

We pray for all who seek to relieve pain, for doctors, nurses and dentists.

We pray for all who work for the redeeming of our world.

By the light of your presence,
fill us with your glory.

As we rejoice in Christ the Light of the world, and know the darkness is conquered,

we pray for friends and loved ones who have passed through the darkness to eternal light.

O Christ, our morning star, when the darkness of this world is past,

let us come before your presence in love and adoration.

By the light of your presence,
fill us with your glory.

THE PEACE

The Light of Christ scatter the darkness from before you.
The Light of Christ guide you into the ways of peace.
The peace of the Lord be always with you
and also with you.

THE BLESSING

Shine as bright lights in this world. Live to show the glory of
God. Let the presence be seen in your life. And the blessing...

The Baptism of Christ
(The First Sunday of Epiphany)

Genesis 1. 1–5 : Ps. 29 : Acts 19. 1–7 : Mark 1. 4–11

Blessed are you, Lord our God,
you have created the heavens and the earth.
Blessed are you, Jesus Christ,
you came among us and were baptized of John.
Blessed are you, Holy life-giving Spirit,
you descend as the dove and you fill us with life.
Blessed are you, Holy Three.
In you we live and move and have our being. **Amen.**

Holy God, holy and Strong One, holy and Mighty One,
we give you thanks for all who are baptized.
We praise you for our own baptism and pray that we may know
that we are always immersed in your presence.
Give your church the power to show that we are members of
Christ, children of God and inheritors of the kingdom of
heaven.
We pray for all who are being prepared for baptism or
confirmation:
for our Godchildren and our Godparents,
for all who have been baptized in this place.
Lord of light,
enlighten all your people.

We pray for justice among the nations:
we remember especially any who are held hostage,
any who suffer from captivity or tyranny.
We pray for all who are slaves to debt
and for the world banks in dealing with the poor nations;
that we all may work for justice and peace.
Lord of light,
enlighten all your people.

We give thanks for all who have been concerned with our
well-being.
We pray for parents and loved ones,
for those who have shared their lives and their faith with us,
for all with whom we work and for all our friends.
Lord of light,
enlighten all your people.

We remember all who are feeling badly bruised,
by illness, by accident or by circumstance.
For all who have suffered spiritually or mentally,
for those with memories that disturb or frighten them.
We remember all who have lost confidence in themselves or in
others.

We pray for the world-weary, the worn and the weak,
that the Lord will give strength to all his people.
Lord of light,
enlighten all your people.

We pray for all who having been baptized have kept the faith;
we pray especially for loved ones departed from
     us ....
May they rejoice in that greater awareness of Father, Son and
     Holy Spirit.
May we rejoice with them as joint inheritors of the kingdom of
     heaven.
Lord of light,
enlighten all your people.

THE PEACE

The Lord gives strength to his people:
the Lord shall give his people the blessing of peace.
The peace of the Lord be always with you
and also with you.

THE BLESSING

God, the Creator, uphold you.
Christ, the Redeemer, enfold you.
The Holy Spirit, the Comforter, guide you.
And the blessing...

The Second Sunday of Epiphany

1 Samuel 3. 1–10 [11–20] : Ps. 139. 1–6, 13–18 (or 1–10) : Revelation 5. 1–10 :
John 1. 43–51

Lord, as you called the disciples,
open our ears to your calling,
open our eyes to your presence,
open our hearts to your love,
that we may hear you, and hearing you may love you,
and loving you may serve you,
whom to serve is perfect freedom;
through Jesus Christ, the lamb of God. **Amen.**

We give you thanks, O Lord, for you have called us to know
    you and to proclaim you.
Lord make us worthy of our calling; may we be faithful to you
    in our discipleship.
We pray that each in their calling may seek to do your will;
that your church may be attentive to your word and seek to do
    your will,
that we may share in the mission and saving work of Christ our
    Lord.
Lord, you are our strength.
You are our salvation.

We pray for all who are seeking to live up to their calling,
for all who are striving to keep the ideals that they see.
We remember all whose work has been frustrated, by evil or by
    accident.

We pray for the underprivileged, the unemployed, for the work
    weary and for the exploited.
Lord, you are our strength.
You are our salvation.

Lord make us aware that you are ever calling us to new
    ventures, new visions:
you call us to extend ourselves.
We pray for the communities to which we belong and in which
    we have an active share.
May we see our daily work as part of our discipleship and
    discipline.
Lord, you are our strength.
You are our salvation.

We pray for all who feel they have laboured in vain,
for all who have toiled hard and achieved nothing,
for those whose world has collapsed around them.
We remember all who have been recently made homeless,
those who have lost loved ones or possessions.
We pray for all who through illness are unable to fulfil
    themselves,
for all who are frustrated with life, all who feel like giving
    up.
Lord, you are our strength.
You are our salvation.

We give thanks for all who have been faithful disciples,
who have heeded your call and obeyed your commands.
We pray for those who now serve you with the saints in glory,
    especially ....
Lord, you are our strength.
You are our salvation.

Grace and peace to you from God our Father and the Lord
Jesus Christ.
The peace of the Lord be always with you
and also with you.

THE BLESSING

God who called you to work with him,
strengthen you by the power of his Spirit,
that you may be worthy of his calling;
and the blessing...

The Third Sunday of Epiphany

Genesis 14. 17–20 : Ps. 128 : Revelation 19. 6–10 : John 2. 1–11

Holy Father, Creator of all things, whose blessed Son turned the
water into wine, grant that he may come to us and change us,
and so transform our lives that in us your glory may be
revealed; through the same Jesus Christ our Lord, to whom
with you and the Holy Spirit be praise and glory for ever and
ever. **Amen.**

Lord, you transformed common water into wine,
may our common lives share in you who are divine:
as you dear Lord have taken on our humanity
may we now partake of your divinity.
Lord, let your church reveal your glory in the world.

We pray today for Christian artists and craftspeople.
Good Lord, transform us,
that we may reveal your glory.

We pray for all that are newly wed, and for those preparing for
marriage.
For all that are discovering a newness in their love for each
other.
We pray for those saving to get married and all who feel that
they cannot afford to marry.
We pray for marriages that have run into difficulties,
for those who are running out of resources, those in debt and
those having homes repossessed;
for all who feel betrayed in their love, for those seeking a
divorce at this time.
We pray for Marriage Guidance Councils and all who seek to
support family life.
Good Lord, transform us,
that we may reveal your glory.

Lord, we pray that your presence may transform our homes,
that our homes may be centres of love, joy and peace.
We pray for friends and loved ones and all who have
transformed our lives by their goodness.
We pray that in our communities we may share and help to
meet each other's needs.
We pray for areas of darkness and deprivation in our
communities.
Good Lord, transform us,
that we may reveal your glory.

We remember all who have run out of resources,
the hungry and thirsty peoples of our world.
We remember the exhausted, and all who can no longer cope on
their own;
all who are struggling to provide for their families and their
basic needs.

We remember all who are in trouble or in sickness,
especially ....
Good Lord, transform us,
that we may reveal your glory.

We rejoice that in you the best is yet to come.
We give thanks for all who have been changed into the glory of
your kingdom.
We pray for loved ones departed from our sight,
especially ....
Good Lord, transform us,
that we may reveal your glory.

THE PEACE

Blessed are those who are called to share in the supper of the
Lamb.
The peace of the Lord be always with you
and also with you.

THE BLESSING

God in his grace and goodness grant you a glimpse of glory;
and the blessing...

The Fourth Sunday of Epiphany

Deuteronomy 18. 15–20 : Ps. 111 : Revelation 12. 1–5a : Mark 1. 21–28

Holy God, give us a deep insight into your ways and the ways of the world, that seeing with a clear vision and having the spirit of discernment, we may be able to stand firm for justice and speak out in truth; through Jesus Christ our Lord, who lives and reigns with you, O Father, and the Holy Spirit, one God, now and for ever. **Amen.**

O Lord, give to us and your whole church
the spirit of wisdom and godly guidance;
that we may discern the times in which we live,
that we may proclaim with relevance the Gospel in all the world.
By your Spirit empower all who preach, to speak clearly and
    with vision.
We pray for all ministers of the word and of the sacraments.
Holy One, hear us.
O God, deliver us.

We pray for rulers and leaders of peoples,
that they may have vision and not neglect the responsibilities
    put on them.
We pray for all who plan for our future, for scientists,
    geneticists, research workers and inventors;
for those who influence our minds through broadcasting or the
    press.
We remember all who have lost vision, and those who lead
    others astray.

Holy One, hear us.
O God, deliver us.

We give you thanks for those who have revealed your presence
    and love to us,
for those who guided us into the ways of truth.
We pray for those who now influence the minds of our young
    people:
for schools, colleges and universities;
for young people who have left home,
for those caught up in crime or in drugs.
Holy One, hear us.
O God, deliver us.

We remember all who are handicapped, the physically infirm,
    the mentally disturbed.
We pray for all who are autistic, all who have difficulties in
    communicating with others;
for those who have lost the power of speech.
We remember those whose minds have been disturbed through
    violence or drugs,
all who have been involved with the occult, all caught up with
    evil.
Holy One, hear us.
O God, deliver us.

We give thanks for your redeeming love and liberating power,
that you free us from the powers of evil, sin and death,
and open up for us the glory of your kingdom.
We pray for all who have died in faith and are now at peace,
    especially ....
May we rejoice with them in your heavenly kingdom.
Holy One, hear us.
O God, deliver us.

THE PEACE

The peace which the world cannot give,
the deep peace of him who stilled the storm;
the peace of the Lord be always with you
and also with you.

THE BLESSING

The Lord of light and love, lead you into the way of peace,
guide you in the way that you are travelling,
protect you from all danger, keep you forever in his care;
and the blessing . . .

Ordinary Time

Proper 1

Sunday between 3 and 9 February inclusive
(if earlier than the Second Sunday before Lent)

———

Isaiah 40. 21–31 : Ps. 147. 1–11 [20c] : 1 Corinthians 9. 16–23 : Mark 1. 29–39

Blessed are you, Lord God of all creation,
for you have brought everything into existence,
you are great and mighty in power.
Be our strength in times of weakness,
uphold us when we are down,
protect us at all times;
through Jesus Christ our Lord. **Amen.**

Lord, we wait, we watch, we long for you.
Renew our powers, refresh our spirits, restore our well-being,
for you give new strength to the faint and power to the
    powerless.
May your church be found working among those who lack
    resources or rights.
May we seek to care for those who cannot care for themselves.
We pray for the lowly and the humiliated.
We pray for relief organizations,
    especially ....

Lord, be to them a tower of strength. Great are you, O Lord,
and mighty is your power.

We pray for the great powers of the world, the strong nations,
and mighty governments:
may their power be used properly that the poor are protected,
the weak are not exploited, and no one is oppressed.
We remember those who have accepted poverty and
vulnerability for the sake of others.
Lord, be to them a tower of strength. Great are you, O Lord,
and mighty is your power.

We give thanks for all who have cared for us in times of
weakness,
for those who have uplifted our spirits and given us new hope.
We pray for our friends and loved ones,
especially any who are finding life difficult at this time.
We pray for any in our community that may feel neglected or
rejected.
Lord, be to them a tower of strength. Great are you, O Lord,
and mighty is your power.

We pray for all who are in weakness of body, mind or spirit,
all who have come to the end of their own resources.
We remember all who are losing their mobility or agility,
those who are losing their memories, and all who have lost their
grip on reality;
for those who no longer trust in anyone, and those who doubt
the love of God;
for all who are caring for loved ones in illness.
Lord, be to them a tower of strength. Great are you, O Lord,
and mighty is your power.

We give thanks that Christ is our healer and our redeemer; he
will not allow us to be lost.
We pray for loved ones departed who are renewed and
refreshed in the love and light of God.

Lord, be to them a tower of strength. Great are you, O Lord,
and mighty is your power.

THE PEACE

Those that wait upon the Lord shall renew their strength.
The peace of the Lord be always with you
and also with you.

THE BLESSING

God, the Holy and Strong One, who gives power to the
    powerless,
who restores the weary, and gives new life to his people,
give you his peace; and the blessing ...

Proper 2

*Sunday between 10 and 16 February inclusive
(if earlier than the Second Sunday before Lent)*

———

2 Kings 5. 1–14 : Ps. 30 : 1 Corinthians 9. 24–27 : Mark 1. 40–45

Praise and thanksgiving to you, O Lord,
for you forgive our sins and heal all our infirmities;
you are our Redeemer and save our lives from destruction.
All that is within me praises your holy Name;
through Jesus Christ, who is alive and reigns with you and the
    Holy Spirit for ever. **Amen.**

Lord, we pray for your church, broken by divisions, separated
   into factions, fallen into disunity.
We pray that it may overcome inborn prejudice, and historic
   animosity,
that we may discover a new unity, a new interdependence.
We pray for all who are striving to bring together those that are
   divided.
Lord, we come to you.
You alone can make us whole.

We pray for the troubled areas of our world:
peoples broken by tyranny and oppression,
societies fractured by violence and suspicion,
nations torn apart by greed and by war;
for all suffering through political divisions or racial hatred,
for all who suffer through ancient suspicions and false fears.
We pray for lepers and for social outcasts.
Lord, we come to you.
You alone can make us whole.

We give you thanks for the wholeness and the wholesomeness
   you offer through a loving family life, through being loved
   and accepted.
We pray for families where there is a breakdown of love or
   trust,
for homes under stress, for all separated from loved ones.
Lord, we come to you.
You alone can make us whole.

We pray for all who are shunned because of their illness or
   colour;
we remember all who are disfigured or whose bodies are
   distorted.
We pray for lepers, those with AIDS, all who are mentally
   handicapped,
and for all who are working for their acceptance and
   well-being.

Lord, we come to you.
You alone can make us whole.

We give thanks for your redeeming love,
for all who have been healed and restored in your kingdom,
all who for the first time rejoice in the fullness of life.
In your kingdom may we share with them in health and in
    wholeness.
Lord, we come to you.
You alone can make us whole.

THE PEACE

The peace of God be in your heart and mind.
The peace of God give you hope and courage.
The peace of God make you whole and holy.
The peace of the Lord be always with you
and also with you.

THE BLESSING

The mighty Father make you strong;
the healing Saviour give you healing;
the Holy Spirit keep you holy;
and the blessing...

Proper 3

Sunday between 17 and 23 February inclusive
(if earlier than the Second Sunday before Lent)

Isaiah 43. 18–25 : Ps. 41 : 2 Corinthians 1. 18–22 : Mark 2. 1–12

Father, in your mercy, forgive us. Restore our relationships.
Make our hearts clean, and renew a right spirit within us;
that we may serve you in goodness and truth;
through Jesus Christ our Lord. **Amen.**

We give thanks for all who have been a strength and a support;
for those who have respected us as people;
for those whose prayers and faith have carried us in time of
    doubt.
Lord, we pray that your church may raise up the fallen,
seek out the lost, be a support to the weary,
strengthen the weak and comfort the sorrowing.
We pray for all who work in rehabilitation and in counselling.
Lord, be merciful to us.
Heal us and raise us up.

Lord, we long for the healing of the nations,
for the time when war will be no more.
We pray that nation may support nation:
that we may discover a new interdependence and unity,
that no peoples may hunger or suffer from poverty,
that no nation may manipulate another or cause them distress.

Lord, be merciful to us.
Heal us and raise us up.

We give thanks for all who have guided and directed us,
for those who have led us into the ways of peace.
We pray for our teachers, for those who set us examples,
for all who maintain the well-being of our society.
We remember our loved ones and our friends.
Lord, be merciful to us.
Heal us and raise us up.

We remember all who have wandered from the truth,
all who have lost their way in life, all who have fallen into
    trouble.
We pray for the lonely and the friendless.
Lord, we pray for all who cannot cope on their own,
for all who are housebound, and for the chronically ill.
We pray for paramedics, district nurses, home helps, for all
    rescue workers.
Lord, be merciful to us.
Heal us and raise us up.

We pray for those who, though lowered into the grave,
have been raised to life with you.
We give thanks for the saints that have gone before us.
We pray for loved ones departed.
Lord, be merciful to us.
Heal us and raise us up.

THE PEACE

The loving Lord will raise up all who are down,
the power of his presence brings peace.
The peace of the Lord be always with you
and also with you.

The Father's love refresh you,
the Son's healing restore you,
the Spirit's power direct you;
and the blessing...

The Second Sunday Before Lent

Proverbs 8. 1, 22–31 : Ps. 104. 24–35 : Colossians 1. 15–20 : John 1. 1–14

Eternal Wisdom, shine in our lives,
that we may delight in you and your light.
Scatter the darkness that is before us,
enlighten our minds and dispel our ignorance,
that we may know you as the true God,
the Maker, Redeemer and Sustainer of all things. **Amen.**

Come, Spirit of God, fill our lives,
fill our minds that we may know you,
fill our hearts that we may love you,
move our wills that we may serve you.
Let our whole being proclaim you.
We pray for the newly baptized, for all being prepared for
    confirmation, and those preparing for ordination;
that your whole church may show forth gifts of the spirit.
Come, Holy Spirit, upon us.
Renew us and direct us.

43

We give thanks for the wonders and mysteries of the world.
We pray today for artists, musicians and talented people.
We pray for all who work in conservation,
that they may work with vision and in gentleness;
for all who are seeking to show a love towards the earth.
Come, Holy Spirit, upon us.
Renew us and direct us.

Lord, be known among the leaders of our community.
Guide with your goodness all making decisions about our
    future.
We pray for planning officers, councillors and politicians:
give them wisdom and a sense of service.
We pray for our own homes and our neighbourhood.
Come, Holy Spirit, upon us.
Renew us and direct us.

We pray for all who walk in darkness, the doubting and the
    despairing.
Lord, we think of those who have suffered through accidents,
those who have endured cruelty, all who have suffered neglect.
We remember any who are captive to bad memories.
We pray today for the terminally ill, for all in a hospice or ill at
    home.
Come, Holy Spirit, upon us.
Renew us and direct us.

We give thanks for all who have shared their wisdom,
all who have left us good examples to follow.
We pray that they, with all the saints and our loved ones
    departed,
may rejoice in the brightness and glory of your kingdom.
Come, Holy Spirit, upon us.
Renew us and direct us.

The grace and goodness of God go with you and surround you
with glory.
The peace of the Lord be always with you
and also with you.

Delight in the Lord always.
Rejoice in the brightness of his presence.
Be renewed by the power of his love.
And the blessing...

The Second Next Before Lent

———

2 Kings 2. 1–12 : Ps. 50. 1–6 : 2 Corinthians 4. 3–6 : Mark 9. 2–9

Loving Lord, let your light shine in our lives,
let its brightness fill our hearts and transfigure us;
that, seeing your glory, we may come to you in awe and wonder,
and gazing upon you may be changed into your likeness,
    moving from glory to glory;
through Jesus Christ our Lord, who with the Father and the
    Holy Spirit is in eternal glory for ever and ever. **Amen.**

Come, Lord of light, transfigure us,
increase our vision and reveal to us your glory.
May your church seek to transform our darkest places with
    your light.

May we seek out the lost and the deprived, the poor and the
   rejected,
and bring them home to you and your love.
We pray for the mission and outreach of the whole church.
Lord, touch us
and transfigure us.

Come, Lord of light, transfigure our towns and our cities.
We pray for areas of danger, for places of vice,
for poor housing and for the street-dwellers.
Lord, transform our places of poverty;
change our attitudes for the better towards each other.
Lord, touch us
and transfigure us.

Lord of light, come transfigure our homes,
that they may be radiant with your presence.
Make them homes of peace and kindliness,
of holiness and hospitality,
of grace and goodness;
that you may be known to be among us.
Lord, touch us
and transfigure us.

Lord of light and love, transfigure our hospitals and nursing
   homes.
We pray for all whose lives have been marred by evil or tragedy.
We pray for all who are downcast or fearful.
We remember all who await a doctor's diagnosis or an
   operation.
We pray for all who seek healing and hope.
Lord, touch us
and transfigure us.

We give thanks for all who have passed beyond death and been
   transformed in your glorious kingdom:
for the saints, for our benefactors, for loved ones departed;

that we like them may come to the fullness of your presence.
Lord, touch us
and transfigure us.

Let the Lord touch you and transform you.
Let the Lord surround you with peace.
The peace of the Lord be always with you
and also with you.

The Lord open your eyes to his presence,
surround you with His great love,
fill your days with his glory;
and the blessing . . .

Lent

The First Sunday of Lent

Genesis 9. 8–17 : Ps. 25. 1–10 : 1 Peter 3. 18–22 : Mark 1. 9–15

Most holy Lord, you were tempted, as we are;
be our strength in times of weakness.
When we fall lift us up, when we are in error direct us.
In all our wanderings, be our guide;
that we may be your faithful people to our life's end. **Amen.**

Lord our God, as we are baptized in your Name,
protect us from all evil and deliver us from all temptation.
May we use this Lent as a time of dedication and renewal.
We pray that your church may stand against evil and seek good.
We remember before you all who have lost faith,
those who no longer pray themselves,
those who find it difficult to trust in you or in anyone.
Lord, we trust in you.
Deliver us from all evil.

We pray for people who have become possessed by greed or
  selfishness,
for all who have become insensitive to the needs of others.
Lord, we remember the exploited peoples:
we pray for those driven off their land and out of their homes;

for all caught up in sectarian violence or in war,
for all who feel inadequate, or unable to cope.
Lord, we trust in you.
Deliver us from all evil.

We give thanks for all who have set us an example of godly
    living,
for people of discipline and dedication.
We pray today for athletes and sportspeople,
for all who learn discipline through their hobbies or work.
We pray for those with whom we work, for our families and
    friends.
Lord, we trust in you.
Deliver us from all evil.

We give you thanks for healers and reconcilers of people.
We pray for all whose relationships have broken down,
for those full of animosity and hatred;
that we all may learn to forgive as we are forgiven.
We pray for all caught up in crime and wickedness.
Lord, we trust in you.
Deliver us from all evil.

We give you thanks and praise for all who have triumphed over
evil and temptation and who now serve you in the peace of
your kingdom. We pray for those who are departed,
especially .... and that at the last we may
share with them in glory.
Lord, we trust in you.
Deliver us from all evil.

THE PEACE

Pray for peace, seek for peace.
Speak of peace, act in peace.
The peace of the Lord be always with you
and also with you.

The Holy and the Strong One, the only true God, scatter the darkness from before you, deliver you from the powers of evil, strengthen you in all goodness, keep you in life eternal; and the blessing...

The Second Sunday of Lent

Genesis 17. 1–7, 15–16 : Ps. 22. 23–31 : Romans 4. 13–25 : Mark 8. 31–38

To you, O Lord, be praise and glory, for the victory of our Lord Jesus Christ over death and hell; in him we are more than conquerors, for he has called us into eternal life. Lord, make us worthy of our calling that we may serve you in love and peace; through Jesus Christ our Lord, who reigns with you and the Holy Spirit, now and for ever. **Amen.**

O God, we come to you with joy, for we are inheritors of the kingdom:
we share with Abraham, Isaac and Jacob in your promises,
we rejoice in your love and your salvation.
As we have received from you, may we bring light and hope to others.
We pray for the wavering in faith and for the weak in spirit.
We pray for lapsed Christians, and for all who have never known you.
We pray for the joy and the mission of your church.
Lord of love and light,
hear us.

You are the hope of all the world.
We pray for better relationships between nations,
for a greater sense of belonging to one great family.
We pray today for the United Nations, for programmes for
    peace,
for a deepening of goodwill among those once at war.
Lord of love and light,
hear us.

Lord, we thank you for all who through good relationships
    have shown your love.
We pray for all whom we love and all who love us.
We pray for the recently engaged and the newly married.
We remember any who are struggling in their relationships.
Lord of love and light,
hear us.

We come with all who have suffered at the hands of others,
all refugees and homeless peoples, dispossessed peoples and
    distraught peoples.
We pray for those afraid of any relationships,
all who can no longer trust anyone, those who cannot trust
    themselves.
We pray for all who are ill and for their loved ones in their
    anxiety.
We pray especially for ....
Lord of love and light,
hear us.

We give thanks for all who have been faithful to you.
We pray for those who now rejoice in your love and peace in its
    fullness.
We pray for loved ones departed,
    especially ....
Lord of love and light,
hear us.

THE PEACE

There is nothing that can separate you from the love and the peace of God.
The peace of the Lord be always with you
and also with you.

THE BLESSING

God the giver of life, give you hope.
Christ the Redeemer, give you peace.
The Holy Spirit who inspires all, give you joy.
And the blessing...

The Third Sunday of Lent

Exodus 20. 1–17 : Ps. 19. [1–6] 7–14 : 1 Corinthians 1. 18–25 : John 2. 13–22

Almighty God, creator of all things,
we give you thanks for the resources of our world,
for the wonders and mysteries of the universe.
Lord, help us to use wisely all you have given to us,
for the benefit of others, for the well-being of the earth, and to
   the glory of your holy Name;
through Jesus Christ our Lord,
who lives and reigns with you and the Holy Spirit,
one God, for ever. **Amen.**

We give you thanks for the beauty and order of our world.
We give thanks for special holy places and for our own church;
through them may we learn awe and respect for your world.
We ask you to guide all leaders of worship, to inspire all
    preachers of the word,
to direct your faithful people in the ways of holiness and peace.
Lord, your will be done on earth,
as it is in heaven.

We pray for all legislators, for those who set standards for us to
    live by.
Guide all those who influence the minds of others:
we pray for broadcasters, the press, for political leaders.
We pray for all dealing in world trade, in commerce or industry.
Give to each the wisdom and will to use properly what you have
    given them.
Lord, your will be done on earth,
as it is in heaven.

We give thanks for those who have shared with us a sense of
    wonder or mystery.
We pray that we may learn to live simply, and to be willing to
    help others to simply live.
Lord, protect us, our homes and loved ones.
Be with all who have been made homeless,
with young people who have recently left home.
Lord, your will be done on earth,
as it is in heaven.

We pray for all who have become possessed by possessions,
for all who are captive to greed and covetousness.
We remember all who have suffered through the selfishness of
    others.
Be a strength, O Lord, to all who have suffered robbery or
    violence,
for all who have faced the murder of a loved one.
We pray for all who have lost their possessions or livelihood,

for those who have become bankrupt.
We pray for all who are ill at this time,
    especially ....
Lord, your will be done on earth,
as it is in heaven.

We give thanks for all who have faithfully obeyed your will,
for all who have worshipped you in the beauty of holiness.
We give thanks for those who founded this church.
We pray for loved ones departed;
grant that we may share with them in your heavenly kingdom.
Lord, your will be done on earth,
as it is in heaven.

THE PEACE

Serve the Lord your God with all your heart, with all your
mind, with all your strength.
The peace of the Lord be always with you
and also with you.

THE BLESSING

God give you grace to do his will.
Christ lead you into the ways of truth.
The Spirit guide you in your dealings.
And the blessing...

The Fourth Sunday of Lent

Numbers 21. 4–9 : Ps. 107. 1–3, 17–22 (*or* 1–9) : Ephesians 2. 1–10 : John 3. 14–21

Lord, we seek to make our home in you, for in you is our hope, in you is our peace. May we abide in you as you are in us. Grant, O Lord, in turning to you we may find new vision, new strength and new love; through Jesus Christ our Lord, who lives and reigns with you and the Holy Spirit, one God, now and for ever. **Amen.**

O gracious Lord, may your church be a home for the weary,
a shelter for the fearful, a strength to the weak,
a place of healing and forgiveness to the troubled and the guilty.
We pray for all who are spiritually hungry,
for all who have lost faith or who have lost hope.
Lord, let your light shine
in our hearts and in your world.

Lord of life, we pray for the starving peoples,
for all without adequate food or shelter,
all who do not have a home to call their own.
We pray for street children, and all who have no one to care for
    them.
Lord, bless the work of all relief agencies,
    especially ....
Lord, let your light shine
in our hearts and in your world.

We come to you, Lord of love.
We give you thanks for our homes and loved ones;
may we not take their love for granted,
may we not be a burden to those with whom we live.
In loving each other may we learn of your love for us.
Lord, let your light shine
in our hearts and in your world.

Loving Lord, we pray for families where there is
    misunderstanding, neglect, violence or apathy.
We pray for homes of poverty and fear.
We remember all who have lost loved ones this week,
all who are caring for loved ones who are ill;
for those parted from their loved ones due to sickness.
Lord, let your light shine
in our hearts and in your world.

Lord, in love you welcome us home,
you come to meet us and lead us to your kingdom.
We pray for all who have the joy of your nearer presence,
for our loved ones departed.
Lord, let your light shine
in our hearts and in your world.

THE PEACE

Walk as children of the light, children of the day, in all goodness and righteousness, and have no dealings with the works of
darkness.
The peace of the Lord be always with you
and also with you.

THE BLESSING

The love of the Father enfold you,
the love of the Saviour uphold you,
the love of the Spirit guide you;
and the blessing...

The Fifth Sunday of Lent
(Passiontide begins)

Jeremiah 31. 31–34 : Ps. 51. 1–12 *or* Ps. 119. 9–16 : Hebrews 5. 5–10 :
John 12. 20–33

Lord Jesus Christ, you were lifted up on the cross for us and for
    our salvation;
help us to triumph over evil and to do good,
to give ourselves to you as you give yourself for us,
and to live and work to your praise and glory. **Amen.**

Lord of the church, may we bring others to know you,
in knowing you to love you,
and in loving you to serve you,
whom to serve is perfect freedom.
We pray for all involved in liberation theology.
Guide and strengthen the mission and outreach of your people.
We pray for missionary societies,
    especially ....
Lord, as you give yourself for us,
let us give ourselves to you.

We pray for leaders of nations, for rulers of peoples,
that they may work with sensitivity and in humility.
We pray for nations emerging from tyranny,
for freedom movements and all who work for liberty.
Lord, as you give yourself for us,
let us give ourselves to you.

We remember all who have been generous to us,
all who have shared their resources and their lives.
We pray for parents who sacrificed for us,
for their giving of time and of attention.
We pray for those who have been denied love,
for all who have been deprived of well-being.
We remember today children taken into care.
Lord, as you give yourself for us,
let us give ourselves to you.

We give thanks for the passion and cross of our Lord, for the
gift of redemption.
We pray for all troubled souls, those anxious about their health,
or their future.
We remember all that are being persecuted for their beliefs or
their principles;
for all who are suffering at this time,
especially ....
Lord, as you give yourself for us,
let us give ourselves to you.

Lord, give comfort to the bereaved, give courage to the dying.
We pray for all who have entered where sorrow and pain are no
more.
We remember loved ones who have entered into eternal life,
and we join with them to sing your praises.
Lord, as you give yourself for us,
let us give ourselves to you.

THE PEACE

Set your troubled hearts at rest, believe in him who has
    conquered death.
Trust in God who gives life eternal.
The peace of the Lord be always with you
and also with you.

THE BLESSING

The Father who created light out of darkness,
the Son who is the light of the world,
the Spirit who enlightens everyone,
the Holy Three be with you,
and scatter the darkness from you;
and the blessing...

Palm Sunday (Liturgy of the Passion)

Isaiah 50. 4–9a : Ps. 31. 9–16 [17–18] : Philippians 2. 5–11 : Mark 14.1—15.47 *or*
Mark 15. 1–39 [40–47]

Holy Father, as Christ entered Jerusalem,
let him enter our lives, let the King of glory come in,
that he may rule in our hearts,
and that we may offer our love and lives to him;
through the same Christ our Lord, who offered his life for us,
and reigns with you and the Holy Spirit, one God, world
    without end. **Amen.**

Christ broken on the cross, we draw near to you,
we come with broken promises and broken dreams,
we come as a church divided and not at unity in itself.
Yet we seek through you to share in salvation,
and to bring others to your saving love.
Lord, as you give yourself to us, may we give ourselves for
    others.
Lord of the cross, we come to you.
You can make us whole.

We pray for nation that is divided against nation,
for peoples that are not at peace with their neighbours;
for all places of discord and dissatisfaction.
Bless, O Lord, the work of the United Nations;
guide all who give themselves in the cause of peace.
We pray for communities torn apart by hatred.
Lord of the cross, we come to you.
You can make us whole.

May we accept you, O Christ, as our King;
let your rule begin in our hearts and homes.
We pray for homes where there is discord;
for homes darkened by deceit and betrayal,
for homes where loyalty and love are divided.
Lord of the cross, we come to you.
You can make us whole.

Lord, be with all who have a difficult week ahead,
the scorned and the rejected, those who face insult or
    degradation.
We remember those who will be persecuted for faith or
    principle,
for those whose spirits will be broken this week.
We pray for the broken-hearted and those with broken
    relationships,

for all who are suffering from any kind of breakdown.
Lord of the cross, we come to you.
You can make us whole.

We give thanks for the holy martyrs of God,
for all who have suffered for others and for truth,
for those who sacrificed for us and are now at rest.
Through your cross and passion may we share with them in
  glory.
Lord of the cross, we come to you.
You can make us whole.

THE PEACE

Jesus is Lord. Jesus is love. Jesus is peace. Jesus is life eternal.
The peace of the Lord be always with you
and also with you.

THE BLESSING

May you find in the Crucified One
the forgiveness of sins,
the renewing power of love,
and the promise of life eternal;
and the blessing . . .

Easter

Easter Day

Acts 10. 34–43 *or* Isaiah 25. 6–9 : Ps. 118. [1–2] 14–24 : 1 Corinthians 15. 1–11 *or* Acts 10. 34–43 : John 20. 1–18 *or* Mark 16. 1–8

Blessed be the risen Lord;
he has broken from the tomb
and opens for us the gate to life eternal.
Blessed be the risen Lord;
he comes to his disciples;
where two or three gather together he is there.
Blessed be the risen Lord:
he comes from the dead with life,
he brings us light and joy and hope.
Blessed be the risen Lord,
Alleluia. Amen.

Holy and everlasting God,
we give you thanks for the resurrection of our Lord Jesus Christ
    from the dead:
in him light triumphs over darkness, life triumphs over death;
in him is our hope and the promise of life eternal.
We pray for all who preach the gospel,
for all who seek to lead others to the risen Lord,
for all who teach of his forgiveness,

for all who have their hope set on eternal life;
that we all may rejoice in the power of the risen Lord.
Jesus, Risen Lord,
open to us the gate of glory.

We look for the coming of peace on earth.
Lord, let us hear that voice which says, 'Peace be with you'.
Let your peace begin in our hearts and in our homes.
Let your peace grow in our communities.
Let your peace reach out into the whole world.
Jesus, Risen Lord,
open to us the gate of glory.

As the risen Lord appeared in the Upper Room,
may he be known to be in our homes and among us.
Lord, destroy all that would lock us in or deny us freedom;
enter our lives that we may live for you.
We pray for our loved ones.
Jesus, Risen Lord,
open to us the gate of glory.

We think of all those who weep today,
those newly separated from loved ones,
all who are caught up in sorrow and are heavy-hearted,
all who are distressed and overwrought.
We remember all who mourn the loss of a loved one.
Lord, wipe away all tears from their eyes,
that they may see you and know life is eternal.
Jesus, Risen Lord,
open to us the gate of glory.

We give you thanks and praise for the gift of eternal life.
We rejoice with your saints in glory,
and we pray for all our loved ones departed this life,
that, free from sorrow and pain, they may be one with you in
    your kingdom.

Jesus, Risen Lord,
open to us the gate of glory.

THE PEACE

The peace of him who triumphs over death,
the peace of him who is the Lord of life,
the peace of him who is the King of glory,
the peace of the Lord be always with you
and also with you.

THE BLESSING

Rejoice, for Christ is risen, he seeks us to rise with Him.
In him is our hope, in life, in death and in all eternity.
Today the risen Lord comes to us with his gift of peace.
And the blessing...

The Second Sunday of Easter

Acts 4. 32–35 : Ps. 133 : 1 John 1.1—2.2 : John 20. 19–31

Christ, our risen Lord, no tomb can keep you,
no door is closed to you, no heart is barred to you,
no mind is shut off from you.
Come lead us out of darkness into light,
out of doubt into faith, out of death into life eternal:
Jesus Christ our risen Lord. **Amen.**

We pray for all who witness to your resurrection,
for those who speak of your presence,
for preachers of the word and ministers of the sacraments;
for those who reveal your presence by the way they live,
for all who live simply that others may simply live.
We pray for all who are in doubt and for all who are seeking
you.
We pray for unity in the church and in the world.
We call to you,
my Lord and my God.

We come today with the oppressed peoples,
with all who have lost their freedom, all who have lost hope.
We pray for all who have been taken hostage,
all who have been imprisoned because of their beliefs;
that in the darkness they may find your love.
We call to you,
my Lord and my God.

We pray for any fellowship to which we belong,
for communities and clubs, for welfare organizations,
for social groups, for those with whom we share our worship.
We give thanks for your appearing in the Upper Room,
and pray for our homes and loved ones.
We call to you,
my Lord and my God.

We remember all who are despairing, those who doubt their
abilities.
We pray for all who lack confidence,
those afraid to trust themselves or others.
We remember all who are lonely, all who are fearful.
We pray for those in sickness, looking to you in hope, O risen
Christ.
We call to you,
my Lord and my God.

Risen Lord, in you is our hope;
in life, in death and to eternity our hope is in you.
We rejoice with all who have entered into the fullness of life
    eternal.
We pray especially for loved ones departed;
may we with them have a share in your eternal kingdom.
We call to you,
my Lord and my God.

THE PEACE

The peace of the eternal Father be about you.
The peace of the risen Lord be within you.
The peace of the Holy Spirit be upon you.
The peace of the Lord be always with you
and also with you.

THE BLESSING

May you find in the risen Lord the way to fullness of life, the
way to joy and peace; and the blessing . . .

The Third Sunday of Easter

Acts 3. 12–19 : Ps. 4 : 1 John 3. 1–7 : Luke 24. 36b–48

Risen Lord, you reveal to us the love and radiance of the Father;
you bring us the peace that passes all understanding.
We rejoice in your presence and in the glory of your resurrection.

Strengthen our faith, O Lord Jesus,
that we may know you live in eternity with the Father and the
   Holy Spirit,
one God, world without end. **Amen.**

Father, we give you thanks for the gift of eternal life.
May we know in our lives that the crucified one is alive and
   comes to us:
turn our doubts and disbelief into awe and wonder,
until we rejoice in the glory and presence of the risen Lord.
We pray for churches struggling at this time,
for those who have lost vision and grown cold in their love;
for Christians who have lost faith or entered into deep doubt.
We pray that the church may witness to your resurrection.
O God our defender,
answer us when we call.

We pray for all who seek to relieve hunger and suffering:
for those who seek to help people rise out of their troubles.
We remember the United Nations and the World Health
   Organization.
We pray for peace-keeping forces and all who work for the
   well-being of others.
We remember especially any whose lives are in danger.
O God our defender,
answer us when we call.

We give you thanks for those who have shared their food and
   faith with us,
for all who have sustained our bodies and our minds,
for those who have cared for the needs of our spirits.
We pray for those who have been deprived of love.
We pray for our homes and our neighbourhood.
O God our defender,
answer us when we call.

We pray for all who hunger for food, for shelter,
for love, for spiritual refreshment;
for the many who feel rejected or lonely:
for the ill who have no one to care for them,
for all finding it hard to cope on their own.
We bring to you friends and loved ones who are ill.
O God our defender,
answer us when we call.

We long for the day when we shall see Christ as he is in his
   glory.
We pray that we may triumph over darkness and death
and share with the faithful in the light of your kingdom.
O God our defender,
answer us when we call.

THE PEACE

The peace of the risen Lord,
the peace of Christ the King,
the peace of the Conqueror of death,
the peace of the Lord be always with you
and also with you.

THE BLESSING

Go out witnessing to the power of the resurrection in the might
of the risen Lord; and the blessing...

The Fourth Sunday of Easter

Acts 4. 5–12 : Ps. 23 : 1 John 3. 16–24 : John 10. 11–18

O God of peace, whose Son, our Lord Jesus Christ, was brought
back from the dead to be the great Shepherd, grant that we may
be led by him out of darkness and death into the fullness of life
eternal; through the same Christ our Lord, who lives and reigns
with you and the Holy Spirit, in all eternity. **Amen.**

Father, we give you thanks for the risen Lord,
the Good Shepherd, who seeks out and saves all who are lost.
We pray for all who are walking in the valley of the shadow at
    this time,
all whose lives are hard or being made hard, for all being
    attacked by evil.
May they know your love and protection.
We remember all who are called to share in the shepherding of
    your people:
we pray for all bishops, priests and deacons,
    especially ....
We pray for the work of the Church Army.
Lord of hosts,
you are our hope and our strength.

We ask you to guide all carers and counsellors.
Strengthen all who are looking after others.
We pray for the Samaritans, for Alcoholics Anonymous,
for all who seek out and befriend the needy.
Lord of hosts,
you are our hope and our strength.

We remember all who have protected us and guided us.
We pray for those who have supported us in times of need,
those who have stayed with us in times of darkness.
We pray for our homes and our loved ones.
Lord of hosts,
you are our hope and our strength.

We come with all who have entered into weakness, darkness or
    trouble this week.
We pray for those who cannot pray for themselves,
for those who have lost memory or reason,
for all who are facing death, especially those who are lonely.
May they know the Good Shepherd is with them.
Lord of hosts,
you are our hope and our strength.

Lord, may we learn to abide in you,
and know that you abide in us.
May we know that nothing separates us from you.
We pray for all who have passed through darkness,
and have entered light and life everlasting.
Lord of hosts,
you are our hope and our strength.

THE PEACE

Abide in him as he abides in you: let his peace fill you and
surround you.
The peace of the Lord be always with you
and also with you.

THE BLESSING

The Mighty Father protect you and enfold you.
The Good Shepherd guide you and revive you.
The Holy Spirit strengthen you and abide in you.
And the blessing...

The Fifth Sunday of Easter

Acts 8. 26–40 : Ps. 22. 25–31 : 1 John 4. 7–21 : John 15. 1–8

God of love, may we abide in your presence and so abide in your love: as we freely receive your love, let us freely share with others all that you have given to us; through Jesus Christ our Lord, who lives and reigns with you and the Holy Spirit, for ever and ever. **Amen.**

Father of all, we pray for your church,
that it may be a caring, loving and accepting church.
We pray for the outreach of your church,
that it may seek out the needy, the outcasts and the rejected:
that love may be revealed in action.
Lord, as you abide in us,
may we abide in you.

We come with sorrow for all who have been denied freedom or
    peace.
We pray for places where communities have been destroyed,
where families have been divided or separated,
for children who have lost contact with their parents.
We remember all who seek to heal that which divides.
Lord, as you abide in us,
may we abide in you.

We give thanks for areas where people can exercise their talents,
where people are free to think and to act without hindrance.
We pray for all who are enriching our world with their gifts.

71

We pray for our families and friends.
Lord, as you abide in us,
may we abide in you.

We think of all whose lives have been marred by their past:
for lives destroyed by bad memories, hatred, guilt or resentment;
for all who are weary of life, who are tired of serving others.
In the power of the risen Lord we ask for renewal, refreshment,
    restoration.
Lord, as you abide in us,
may we abide in you.

Lord of life and love, we praise you for all who have borne fruit
    in your service,
for all who have forwarded your kingdom,
for all who have shared their love and goodness.
We pray for all our loved ones departed.
Lord, as you abide in us,
may we abide in you.

THE PEACE

All who say they love God must love their fellow humans;
all who seek peace must share the peace that is offered.
The peace of the Lord be always with you
and also with you.

THE BLESSING

Abide in the power of the Almighty,
abide in the love of the Saviour,
abide in the fellowship of the Spirit,
that you may bear much fruit;
and the blessing...

The Sixth Sunday of Easter

Acts 10. 44–48 : Ps. 98 : 1 John 5. 1–6 : John 15. 9–17

Lord, as you have chosen us, empower and equip us; make us worthy of our calling that we may reveal your love and show forth your glory; through Jesus Christ our Lord, who with you and the Holy Spirit abides for ever. **Amen.**

We rejoice that you have called us to be sons and daughters of
   God,
you have given us a faith that in you conquers all things.
Bless, O Lord, all who are seeking to live by what they believe,
all who long to hear your word and do your will.
We pray for all in their ministry and vocation,
especially any going through a time of trial or temptation.
Lord of all creation,
your will be done.

Guide all leaders in industry and commerce;
may the goods of this world be neither hoarded nor squandered.
We pray that there may be a fairer distribution of wealth.
We pray for all who are ill treated in the world of trade.
Lord of all creation,
your will be done.

Lord, we rejoice that you have called us to know you,
you have called us to love you,
you have called us to serve you.
May we reveal our calling, love and service in all our dealings.

Lord, bless and protect our homes and loved ones.
Lord of all creation,
your will be done.

Lord of love, be a comfort to the sorrowing,
be a strength to the weak, give hope to all who are dying.
We pray for all who have been injured this week,
all who have fallen into illness or disability,
for those who can no longer cope on their own;
that each in their trouble may know your love.
Lord of all creation,
your will be done.

We pray for our loved ones departed.
We look forward to the time when we shall see, and know,
when we shall know and love,
when we shall love and enjoy you for ever,
when we shall share with your saints in glory.
Lord of all creation,
your will be done.

THE PEACE

Peace be in your dealings.
Peace be in your thinking.
Peace be in your life.
The peace of the Lord be always with you
and also with you.

THE BLESSING

Love the Lord your God, with all your heart and mind and
strength:
your neighbour as yourself; and the blessing...

Ascension Day

———

Acts 1. 1–11 *or* Daniel 7. 9–14 : Ps. 47 *or* Ps. 93 : Ephesians 1. 15–23 *or*
Acts 1. 1–11 : Luke 24. 44–53

Glory to the King of kings. Glory to the Lord of lords. Glory to
  him who has ascended.
O risen and ascended Christ, all authority in heaven and earth is
  yours.
We proclaim you as our Lord.
We offer you our love.
We give you our whole lives.
Lord, may we enter into your kingdom and be with you in
  glory,
where you are with the Father and the Holy Spirit, one God for
  ever. **Amen.**

Glory to you, O God, for Christ risen and ascended.
King of kings, come rule in our hearts,
make us part of your kingdom.
Ascended Christ, send us out to proclaim you to the nations,
let your church reveal your glory.
In your power let us uplift all who are down and despairing.
We pray for all who have lost vision or hope.
Your kingdom come in us,
as it is in heaven.

May we let the King of Glory rule in our lives,
that the kingdoms of the world may become his kingdom.
We pray for a reign of peace and love upon the earth,

a deepening fellowship between nations and peoples:
for a time when no one will be exploited and no one neglected.
Your kingdom come in us,
as it is in heaven.

Lord, let us see that your love rules in our hearts and homes.
We pray for all who give hospitality to others,
for those caring for visitors and strangers;
we pray for hotels and bed and breakfast accommodation.
We remember those who are homeless.
Your kingdom come in us,
as it is in heaven.

We pray for all who have fallen into sin and evil;
for all who have fallen upon bad times, for all who have fallen
    into sickness,
that in you they may be uplifted and rise above that which
    would bring them down.
We pray for loved ones who are ill,
and for all who have the care of them.
Your kingdom come in us,
as it is in heaven.

We rejoice with all who are in the fullness of your kingdom,
with all who have triumphed over suffering and death,
and pray we may share with them in your glory.
Your kingdom come in us,
as it is in heaven.

THE PEACE

The God of heaven and earth give you peace.
Christ the risen and ascended Lord give you peace.
The Spirit who fills your life give you peace.
The peace of the Lord be always with you
and also with you.

Christ the King of Glory, who has ascended into heaven,
open your eyes to behold him in majesty,
open your hearts to receive him in love,
and draw you into the fullness of his kingdom;
and the blessing . . .

The Seventh Sunday of Easter (Sunday after Ascension Day)

Acts 1. 15–17, 21–26 : Ps. 1 : 1 John 5. 9–13 : John 17. 6–19

Holy Spirit of God,
we watch for you, we wait for you,
we look for you, we long for you.
Come Holy Spirit, renew us, refresh us, restore us and inspire
us, that we may live and work to your glory;
through Jesus Christ our Lord, who with you, O Spirit, are with
the Father, one God for ever. **Amen.**

We give you thanks and praise for all teachers of the faith,
for those who have proclaimed your word and taught of your
glory.
We pray for all being prepared for baptism, for all confirmation
classes.
We remember those being prepared for ordination,
that we with them may learn to wait upon the Spirit,
and to become witnesses of the resurrection.

We pray for all who are struggling with their faith,
for all who are in doubt about their vocation.
Spirit of God, we wait upon you.
Strengthen us and restore us.

Strengthen, O Lord, all who work to meet the needs of the
    world.
We pray that talents may not be lost through neglect or
    discouragement.
We remember all who work in commerce and in industry.
We pray for farmers and agricultural workers,
for fishermen and all who work upon the sea.
Spirit of God, we wait upon you.
Strengthen us and restore us.

O Lord, guide the communities to which we belong into peace;
that there may be peace in our streets,
peace in our homes, peace in all our dealings;
that our loved ones may live and abide in peace.
Spirit of God, we wait upon you.
Strengthen us and restore us.

For all who are waiting for clinical results and tests,
those who await a doctor's diagnosis or an operation.
Support all who wait by an ailing loved one,
all near to and awaiting the hour of death.
Spirit of God, we wait upon you.
Strengthen us and restore us.

We give thanks for your renewing powers,
and we pray for our loved ones departed,
that in you they may know newness of life.
Spirit of God, we wait upon you.
Strengthen us and restore us.

All who wait upon the Lord will renew their strength.
The peace of the Lord be always with you
and also with you.

THE BLESSING

The Holy and Mighty God protect you from all evil,
Christ the King deliver you from all darkness,
the Holy Spirit guide you into ways of peace;
and the blessing...

Day of Pentecost

Acts 2. 1–21 *or* Ezekiel 37. 1–14 : Ps. 104. 24–34, 35b (*or* 24–36) :
Romans 8. 22–27 *or* Acts 2. 1–21 : John 15. 26–27; 16. 4b–15

Come, Holy Spirit, come upon us,
come around us, come within us;
come to lead us, come to guide us,
that we may work in your power,
and rest in your presence:
through Jesus Christ our Lord,
who lives and reigns with you and the Father,
one God for ever. **Amen.**

Holy Spirit, giver of all good gifts,
come into our darkness as light,
come as the wind to refresh us and uplift us.

Come as joy to disperse our sorrows,
come as power to enable us and encourage us.
Come as love and revive your church,
that we may show and share your gifts,
that we may reach out in love through your grace.
The Lord is here.
His Spirit is with us.

Come, Holy Spirit, direct our rulers: fill our leaders with talent
    and discernment;
inspire our artists and musicians, writers and craftspeople.
Come, Spirit of God, give peace and unity to the nations;
come, renew the face of the earth.
The Lord is here.
His Spirit is with us.

Come, Holy Spirit, fill our homes,
set our hearts on fire with the warmth of your love;
come stir our minds and inspire us to do new things.
Guide us in our relationships with each other,
and draw us together in your fellowship of love and joy.
The Lord is here.
His Spirit is with us.

We come with all who are weary, all whose hope has dried up;
we come with the despairing, the despondent,
and all who are dis-spirited, with depressed and oppressed
    peoples.
We pray for all who have become very weak,
for all who are infirm and cannot cope on their own.
O Spirit of God, stir up your power and come among us.
The Lord is here.
His Spirit is with us.

Spirit of God, you breathe life into dry bones,
you give new life to your people;
we pray for our loved ones departed,
    especially ....

The Lord is here.
His Spirit is with us.

The Lord sends out his Spirit and renews the face of the earth.
The peace of the Lord be always with you
and also with you.

THE BLESSING

The Spirit of God come upon you,
fill you with peace and love,
guide you in all that you do;
and the blessing...

Ordinary Time

Trinity Sunday

Isaiah 6. 1–8 : Ps. 29 : Romans 8. 12–17 : John 3. 1–17

The Trinity protecting me;
the Father be over me,
the Saviour be under me,
the Spirit be within me.
The Holy Three enfolding me,
ever more about me.
Holy God, holy and Strong One, holy and Mighty One,
You give us life, you give us love, you give us yourself;
help us to give our lives, our love, ourselves to you. **Amen.**

We pray for pilgrims and seekers, for all new in the faith.
We long for a deeper unity and fellowship within the church.
Lord, give to your people
the blessing of peace.

We pray for your creation that groans for salvation:
for areas spoiled and desecrated by greed or insensitivity,
for peoples misused, exploited and abused by others,
for all places of deprivation or great poverty,
for all who suffer from war or oppression.
Lord, give to your people
the blessing of peace.

We give you thanks for all who have shared their lives with us.
We pray for our homes, our loved ones,
for friends who have guided us, all who have been an example
   to us.
We pray for young people leaving home for the first time,
for anyone who has had to leave their home because of illness.
Lord, give to your people
the blessing of peace.

We pray for all who are disturbed:
for the mentally ill, for people with schizophrenia,
for all who have lost their grip on reality.
We remember the restless and the weary,
all who are not at peace with themselves or the world.
Lord, be with each in their troubles and with all who care for
   them.
Lord, give to your people
the blessing of peace.

Praise you for all who have come into the peace of your nearer
   presence:
for the saints in glory, and for our loved ones departed.
Lord, give to your people
the blessing of peace.

THE PEACE

The peace of God the Creator,
the peace of Christ the Redeemer,
the peace of the Spirit the Life-giver,
the peace of the One and of the Three;
the peace of the Lord be always with you
and also with you.

God, the Maker of all, surround you with his love,
Christ, the Saviour of all, keep you in his love,
the Holy Spirit, the Sanctifier, fill you with his love,
The love of the Holy Three be within you and about you;
and the blessing...

Proper 4

Sunday between 29 May and 4 June inclusive (if after Trinity Sunday)

———

Track 1
1 Samuel 3. 1–10 [11–20]
Ps. 139. 1–6, 13–18
2 Corinthians 4. 5–12
Mark 2.23—3.6

Track 2
Deuteronomy 5. 12–15
Ps. 81. 1–10
2 Corinthians 4. 5–12
Mark 2.23 — 3.6

God of light and power and glory, we rejoice in your light,
we live by your power, we look for your glory.
Open our eyes to behold your presence,
that we may give ourselves to you;
through Jesus Christ our Lord,
who lives and reigns with you and the Holy Spirit,
one God for ever and ever. **Amen.**

We give you thanks for the light that is revealed to us in the face
of our Lord Jesus Christ.
Lord, enlighten your church where its vision is dim and the light
of the gospel is nearly gone out.
We pray for spiritual renewal, for an increase in vision and hope.

We remember all who are prophets and visionaries today.
The Lord is our hope.
God is our joy and strength.

Lord, direct all who are seeking to improve the world.
We pray for peace-makers, for relief agencies,
for all involved in scientific research,
for all who hunger and thirst for righteousness;
that the poor may receive what is needful for their welfare.
The Lord is our hope.
God is our joy and strength.

We give thanks for all who led us to you,
all who shared their insight and knowledge,
all who kept the lamp of faith burning.
We pray for those who have maintained the church,
for those who have been accepting and understanding.
The Lord is our hope.
God is our joy and strength.

We pray for all who have entered into weakness,
into sadness or into trouble this week,
all who have been injured in accidents,
those suffering from a stroke or paralysis,
all on a life-support machine at this time.
We pray for the afflicted, the perplexed,
the persecuted and all who feel forsaken.
The Lord is our hope.
God is our joy and strength.

We rejoice that the afflicted will know affection,
the perplexed will discover your purpose,
the persecuted will come to your peace,
the forsaken will be enfolded in love,
in the fullness of your kingdom.
We pray for loved ones departed.
The Lord is our hope.
God is our joy and strength.

THE PEACE

Power belongs to God, it does not come from us;
in him is our joy, our hope and our peace.
The peace of the Lord be always with you
and also with you.

THE BLESSING

Let the joy of the Presence, the vision of his glory,
the hope of his kingdom, strengthen you and fill you with peace;
and the blessing . . .

Proper 5

Sunday between 5 and 11 June inclusive (if after Trinity Sunday)

Track 1	Track 2
1 Samuel 8. 4–11 [12–15] 16–20	Genesis 3. 8–15
[11. 14–15]	Ps. 130
Ps. 138	2 Corinthians 4.13—5.1
2 Corinthians 4.13—5.1	Mark 3. 20–35
Mark 3. 20–35	

Glory be to God the Father Almighty,
who raised our Lord Jesus Christ from the dead.
Glory be to him who will raise us up
and bring us into the fullness of his kingdom.
Father, we give our lives to you,
that you may take us and transform us;
through Jesus Christ our Lord,

86

who is alive and reigns with you and the Holy Spirit,
one God for ever and ever. **Amen.**

We give you thanks for all who have remained faithful to you,
for all who have seen beyond the temporary to the eternal,
for saints and martyrs who have been our inspiration.
We pray for the church where it is being persecuted,
for all Christians afflicted or tortured for their faith.
Lord, be a strength to all who are losing hope,
to the faint-hearted and the fearful.
Lord, we call to you.
Hear us and answer us.

God of peace, we pray for countries broken by war,
for peoples facing ethnic violence and hatred,
for all who are being discriminated against.
We remember those being robbed of homes,
of their land or their livelihood.
Lord, we call to you.
Hear us and answer us.

We give thanks for those who have protected us,
who have shielded us from harm or evil,
who have enriched our lives by their goodness.
We pray for the police and the fire service,
for all upon whom our security depends.
Lord, we call to you.
Hear us and answer us.

We pray for areas where lives are wasting away,
for the poor, the homeless and the refugee;
for all who suffer from mental illness, the disturbed and the
    violent;
for all who have lost the will to live, and for the suicidal.
Lord, we call to you.
Hear us and answer us.

Lord, extend our vision, may we look beyond what we see to
the eternal.
We pray for all who see you in that glory which is beyond
measure;
we remember loved ones departed ....
Lord, we call to you.
Hear us and answer us.

THE PEACE

The Mighty God will raise us up with Jesus,
and bring us to behold his great glory.
The peace of the Lord be always with you
and also with you.

THE BLESSING

Do not lose heart or be afraid, hold fast to that which is good,
look to that which is eternal; and the blessing...

Proper 6

Sunday between 12 and 18 June inclusive (if after Trinity Sunday)

Track 1
1 Samuel 15.34—16.13
Ps. 20
2 Corinthians 5. 6–10 [11–13] 14–17
Mark 4. 26–34

Track 2
Ezekiel 17. 22–24
Ps. 92. 1–4, 12–15 (*or* 1–8)
2 Corinthians 5. 6–10 [11–13] 14–17
Mark 4. 26–34

Lord God, Almighty, rule in our hearts:
direct our decisions, guide our actions,
let your kingdom grow in us,
that we may live and work to your praise and glory;
through Jesus Christ our Lord,
who is alive and reigns with you and the Holy Spirit,
one God for ever and ever. **Amen.**

As we rejoice in the gospel, we pray for all who spread the
  Good News,
for evangelists and preachers, for Sunday school teachers,
for all the laity in their sharing of the faith.
We pray for all who produce Bibles,
and those who help us to understand your holy word.
Lord, may your church grow in holiness, in outreach and in
  number.
Lord, hear us.
Lord, graciously hear us.

We give thanks for the written and spoken word.
We pray for publishers and broadcasters,

for politicians and leaders of nations.
We pray for those who through meetings influence our lives,
for all who make decisions about our world and our future.
Lord, hear us.
Lord, graciously hear us.

We remember with affection all who have helped us to grow,
physically, mentally or spiritually.
We pray for teachers who have taught us,
for churches that have enriched us,
for loved ones who have sustained us.
We pray for all whose growth is stunted,
for all who lack love or attention,
for all who suffer from neglect or abuse.
Lord, hear us.
Lord, graciously hear us.

Loving Father, sustain all whom the world has hurt,
those whose lives are denied natural growth,
who suffer from poverty, oppression or circumstance.
We remember all who are frustrated by weakness,
sickness or any other disability.
For friends and loved ones in need ....
Lord, hear us.
Lord, graciously hear us.

Blessed are you, Lord God, for you give us the victory.
We give you thanks for all who are in sorrow and pain no more;
all who have triumphed over death and the grave are in life
    eternal.
We pray for loved ones departed.
Lord, hear us.
Lord, graciously hear us.

Live not to yourself alone, live for the good of others, live to the
glory of God.
The peace of the Lord be always with you
and also with you.

THE BLESSING

God give you grace to grow in holiness,
to extend your vision, to increase your faith,
to draw nearer to him;
and the blessing...

Proper 7

Sunday between 19 and 25 June inclusive (if after Trinity Sunday)

Track 1
1 Samuel 17. [1a, 4–11, 19–23] 32–49
Ps. 9. 9–20
or: 1 Samuel 17.57—18.5, 10–16
Ps. 133
2 Corinthians 6. 1–13
Mark 4. 35–41

Track 2
Job 38. 1–11
Ps. 107. [1–3] 23–32
2 Corinthians 6. 1–13
Mark 4. 35–41

Jesus Christ, Saviour and Prince of peace,
still us, O Lord, as you stilled the storm,
calm us, O Lord, and keep us from harm.
Let all the troubles within us cease.
Enfold us Lord in your deep peace. **Amen.**

We give you thanks for the endurance of the Church.
For all unafraid of death as they look to the resurrection.
We pray for Christians witnessing amid afflictions, hardships
and calamities;
for all who are being persecuted for their faith,
for those who have suffered beatings, imprisonment or scorn,
for all who witness to your love in difficult places.
Lord, bless your people
and give us life for evermore.

Lord of the earth and sea, protect all who work upon the seas:
all fishermen, and seafaring peoples;
we pray for the Royal Navy and for the Merchant Navy,
for those who man lifeboats or work on oil rigs.
We pray for all whose lives are endangered by storm and flood.
Lord, bless your people
and give us life for evermore.

We give thanks for all who provide our food,
all who protect us, and shield us from harm.
We pray today for our own homes and loved ones,
and we remember any who have recently lost their homes or
their livelihood.
Lord, bless your people
and give us life for evermore.

Lord of all power, be with all who are being overwhelmed,
protect all who are in the storms of life,
all who are facing hardship and danger,
all who are having sleepless nights,
all exhausted and hungry peoples.
We pray for the fearful and the anxious,
that the storm-tossed may know your peace.
Lord, bless your people
and give us life for evermore.

We give thanks for all who have passed through life's storms
and are now at peace in your presence.
We pray for loved ones departed,
especially for ....
Lord, bless your people
and give us life for evermore.

THE PEACE

Accept the peace that our Lord gives.
The deep peace of the Prince of peace be within you and about
you.
The peace of the Lord be always with you
and also with you.

THE BLESSING

Let the power and peace of the presence of God fill your life and
be at work within you; and the blessing...

Proper 8

Sunday between 26 June and 2 July inclusive

———

Track 1
2 Samuel 1. 1, 17–27
Ps. 130
2 Corinthians 8. 7–15
Mark 5. 21–43

Track 2
Wisdom of Solomon 1. 13–15; 2. 23–24
Canticle: Lamentations 3. 23–33 *or* Ps. 30
2 Corinthians 8. 7–15
Mark 5. 21–43

O God, you created us in love and for eternity,
and you gave your Son that we should not perish but have
    everlasting life;
as you give us life and love, as you give us yourself,
help us to give our lives, our love, ourselves to you;
through Jesus Christ our Lord,
who is alive and reigns with you and the Holy Spirit,
one God for ever and ever. **Amen.**

Lord of life, may your church proclaim your saving power.
Strengthen all who seek to extend our lives and our vision.
Bless all who are preachers or teachers in your church.
We pray for church schools and colleges.
Lord, forgive us where we are divided, and make us one:
we pray for all who are working for unity and peace.
Lord, we come to you.
You can make us whole.

Lord of peace, be with all suffering from war,
all divided peoples, all separated from loved ones, families and
    friends.

We pray for refugees and displaced persons,
for those living in slums and those living on the streets,
for all living in places that are not wholesome or life-giving.
Lord, we come to you.
You can make us whole.

Lord, as you have given to us in abundance, may we seek to
    share with any in need.
In our community, help us to overcome divisions,
root out all that would poison or spoil our well-being.
We pray for families that are divided,
for all suffering from factions and broken relationships.
Lord, we come to you.
You can make us whole.

Lord of love, we pray for all who are seen as untouchable,
for people who are rejected and feared by others.
Be a presence of support to all who are severely handicapped,
to the mentally disturbed, to those suffering from leprosy and to
    all who have AIDS.
Comfort all who lack affection;
we pray for the broken-hearted and the broken-spirited.
Lord, we come to you.
You can make us whole.

Give strength to all who are watching by beds of sickness,
all who are caring for loved ones who are dying.
Comfort all who have lost loved ones this week.
Lord, we pray that our loved ones departed may arise to life
    eternal in Christ.
Lord, we come to you.
You can make us whole.

THE PEACE

Come to the Lord all who are weary, for he will give you rest.
The peace of the Lord be always with you
and also with you.

THE BLESSING

The Lord of light and love, the giver of life eternal, fill your lives
with his grace and goodness; and the blessing . . .

Proper 9

Sunday between 3 and 9 July inclusive

———

Track 1	Track 2
2 Samuel 5. 1–5, 9–10	Ezekiel 2. 1–5
Ps. 48	Ps. 123
2 Corinthians 12. 2–10	2 Corinthians 12. 2–10
Mark 6. 1–13	Mark 6. 1–13

O Lord of light and vision, open our eyes to behold your
presence, to perceive your love and to see your purpose for us;
that rejoicing in your presence and strengthened by your love
we may do your will and become what you have called us to be;
through Jesus Christ our Lord, who is alive and reigns with you
and the Holy Spirit, one God for ever and ever. **Amen.**

Lord, come into our weakness with your power,
touch our eyes that they may behold your glory.
Grant, O Lord, that your church may lead many to you;

we pray for the outreach and mission of the faithful,
for all who teach the faith and pass it on by example,
for all who are quiet witnesses to what they believe,
for each in their vocation and ministry.
Lord, have mercy,
have mercy on us.

God of love, guide communities which are growing in
    fellowship and in understanding.
Direct all who are seeking to build up community life.
We pray for local projects ....
for local leaders.
We seek your blessing upon this land and upon your world.
Lord, have mercy,
have mercy on us.

Father, strengthen our bonds of love.
We pray that children may be brought up with respect and
    freedom,
that each may have proper spiritual nourishment.
We pray for all who are undervalued or taken for granted,
for the unnoticed workers in our community,
for refuse collectors and street cleaners.
Lord, have mercy,
have mercy on us.

We pray for all who have suffered hardship, persecution or
    calamity this week:
for those injured in accidents or suddenly taken ill.
We pray for all with the gifts of healing, for all who anoint the
    sick.
Lord, have mercy,
have mercy on us.

Lord, give life to our loved ones departed,
give them joy and peace in your eternal kingdom.
Lord, have mercy,
have mercy on us.

The peace of Christ in your heart,
the peace of Christ in your mind,
the peace of Christ in your life,
the peace of the Lord be always with you
and also with you.

THE BLESSING

The presence of the Father enfold you,
the peace of the Saviour be upon you,
the power of the Spirit be within you;
and the blessing...

Proper 10

Sunday between 10 and 16 July inclusive

Track 1	Track 2
2 Samuel 6. 1–5, 12	Amos 7. 7–15
Ps. 24	Ps. 85. 8–13
Ephesians 1. 3–14	Ephesians 1. 3–14
Mark 6. 14–29	Mark 6. 14–29

Blessed are you, God and Father of our Lord Jesus Christ, you
have blessed us with every spiritual blessing; enable us by your
power to be true to our calling and live holy and blameless
before you all our days; through Jesus Christ our Lord, who is
alive and reigns with you and the Holy Spirit, for ever and ever.
Amen.

We offer ourselves with all who have lived holy and dedicated
 lives;
Lord, make us to be numbered with your saints.
We give thanks for the life and witness of John the Baptist.
We pray for all who have been imprisoned for their faith,
for all who at this time are facing persecution or danger,
for all who stand firmly for freedom and justice.
Show us your mercy, O Lord,
and grant us your salvation.

O Lord, support all who seek to support others,
all who care for the homeless and poverty-stricken,
all who work with prisoners or outcasts.
Give courage to all who seek to live in simplicity,
to all who sacrifice themselves that others may live.
We pray for monastic communities, for monks and nuns,
for all leading lives of quiet dedication.
Show us your mercy, O Lord,
and grant us your salvation.

We pray for all who speak out for the communities to which we
 belong,
for councillors and community workers.
Bless our homes, our families and friends,
support with your love all who sustain family life.
We pray for families that are in trouble at this time.
Show us your mercy, O Lord,
and grant us your salvation.

God, lover of the poor, be a strength to the persecuted.
We pray for those who lack the resources they need,
for communities with poor medical supplies,
all who lack food or shelter, any denied a proper education.
We remember all in sickness, and pray especially
 for . . . .
Show us your mercy, O Lord,
and grant us your salvation.

Glory to you, O Lord, for you give us the victory,
in you we triumph over death and have life eternal.
We pray for the saints who stood firm and witnessed to your
love;
we pray for all our loved ones departed.
Show us your mercy, O Lord,
and grant us your salvation.

THE PEACE

In him, who is our peace, we have perfect redemption,
the forgiveness of sins and the riches of his grace.
The peace of the Lord be always with you
and also with you.

THE BLESSING

God give you grace, to become the people he has called you to be,
that you may live and work to his praise and glory;
and the blessing . . .

Proper 11

Sunday between 17 and 23 July inclusive

Track 1
2 Samuel 7. 1–14a
Ps. 89. 20–37
Ephesians 2. 11–22
Mark 6. 30–34, 53–56

Track 2
Jeremiah 23. 1–6
Ps. 23
Ephesians 2. 11–22
Mark 6. 30–34, 53–56

God of peace, whose Son Jesus Christ returned from the dead to become the Great Shepherd of your sheep, guide us into the ways of peace and mercy, equip us to do everything that is good and build us up to be a holy dwelling-place for you our God; through the same Christ, who with you and the Holy Spirit are one God, now and for ever. **Amen.**

Holy Father, empower all whom you have called to be bishops,
   pastors and teachers to be good shepherds of your flock.
Give them wisdom and vision in the leading of your people.
We pray for any who are seeking out the straying and the lost,
those who are offering new hope and courage to the despairing.
Faithful Shepherd,
hear us and guide us.

Give guidance to all who seek to guide or reconcile others;
protect all who are working with divided peoples,
all peace-keeping forces and those who seek to maintain order.
Direct all who work as Samaritans or in marriage guidance.
Faithful Shepherd,
hear us and guide us.

Surround with your love all who are having difficulties in their relationships.
We pray for all who are feeling betrayed or neglected,
for all who are suffering from marriage breakdown,
for children of broken homes or homes of hatred and violence.
Faithful Shepherd,
hear us and guide us.

Good Shepherd, be with all who are harassed and helpless,
all who feel alienated or hostile,
those like sheep without a shepherd.
We remember all who have lost their way,
all fallen into vice and wickedness;
that all may know the love and care of the Good Shepherd.
Faithful Shepherd,
hear us and guide us.

We rejoice with all who are in the safety of your keeping in your kingdom, for all the saints in glory.
We pray for our loved ones departed, and that we may come to share with them in eternal life.
Faithful Shepherd,
hear us and guide us.

THE PEACE

Christ the Good Shepherd comes with peace to those who are near and to those who are far off.
The peace of the Lord be always with you
and also with you.

The leading of the Good Shepherd bring you into ways of peace and light,
protect you through the dark valley, and keep you in love and life eternal;
and the blessing ...

Proper 12

Sunday between 24 and 30 July inclusive

Track 1	Track 2
2 Samuel 11. 1–15	2 Kings 4. 42–44
Ps. 14	Ps. 145. 10–18
Ephesians 3. 14–21	Ephesians 3. 14–21
John 6. 1–21	John 6. 1–21

Lord, throughout our lives we hunger and thirst for you, we long for you, we look for you; nothing in this world can fill us unless you come to us. Lord we will perish, we will sink amid the storms unless you uphold us, come enfold us in your peace, O Christ our Lord, who with the Father and the Holy Spirit are one God, for ever. **Amen.**

Lord, in all of life you provide for us,
you feed us, you support us, you love us,
you fill us with the glory of your presence;
Lord, as we have greatly received, may we share with others.
May we share the Good News and share our prosperity.
We pray for relief organizations,
    especially ....

103

Lord, you open your hands
and you meet our needs.

Creator God, bless all who provide us with our needs:
we pray for the farmers and the fishermen of our world,
especially in areas where crops have failed,
for all who have suffered through storms and disasters.
We remember all who transport food and all who sell it in
   shops.
Lord, you open your hands
and you meet our needs.

Lord, we pray for all who are without resources,
homes where there is hunger and poverty,
places where people suffer from malnutrition.
all peoples who are greatly in debt,
for those who have had homes or possessions repossessed.
Lord, you open your hands
and you meet our needs.

We pray for all who are storm-tossed at this time,
for all who are struggling to survive.
We pray for friends and loved ones who are ill,
for all who can no longer cope alone,
for the fearful and the anxious.
Lord, you open your hands
and you meet our needs.

We remember all who have gone beyond the storms of life and
   are now at peace in your eternal presence.
We pray for friends and loved ones departed.
Lord, you open your hands
and you meet our needs.

THE PEACE

May you know in your lives the love of Christ, that surpasses all knowledge,
and so be filled with the love and fullness of God.
The peace of the Lord be always with you
and also with you.

THE BLESSING

Now to our great God, who is able to accomplish in us far more than we ask or can even imagine, to him be glory for ever and ever; and the blessing . . .

Proper 13

Sunday between 31 July and 6 August inclusive

Track 1
2 Samuel 11.26—12.13a
Ps. 51. 1–12
Ephesians 4. 1–16
John 6. 24–35

Track 2
Exodus 16. 2–4, 9–15
Ps. 78. 23–29
Ephesians 4. 1–16
John 6. 24–35

O Lord our God, you give us the true bread that comes down from heaven, even your Son Jesus Christ our Lord; grant that as we receive him into our lives we may be filled with the fullness of his love and abide in him as he abides in us; through the same Christ our Lord, who lives and reigns with you and the Holy Spirit, one God for ever. **Amen.**

We give you thanks for Holy Communion,
and pray that we may live in Christ as he is in us.
Bless all who minister the sacraments and care for your people.
We pray for all who are being prepared for confirmation or
baptism.
Guide all who are working in mission and outreach.
Good Shepherd, lead us,
and help us to do your will.

Blessed are you, Lord God, for you give gifts to your people.
We pray for social workers, carers, home helps,
for all who seek to meet the needs of others within their
community.
We pray especially today for those who live in deserts, in the
barren areas of the world;
for places where crops are meagre or have failed.
Good Shepherd, lead us,
and help us to do your will.

Lord, giver of all good things, we give you thanks for all who
have provided for us.
We pray for our homes and our loved ones, for all for whom we
ought to provide;
Lord, that we may be sensitive and caring in our community.
Good Shepherd, lead us,
and help us to do your will.

God of all power and might, comfort all who have run out of
power,
all who lack energy or whose abilities are failing.
We pray for those who are weak through hunger and neglect,
for all who have become ill, and all who care for them.
Good Shepherd, lead us,
and help us to do your will.

You are the God who heals and restores.
We give thanks for all who have entered into newness of life in
your kingdom.

We pray for loved ones who serve you now in glory.
Good Shepherd, lead us,
and help us to do your will.

THE PEACE

Make every effort to maintain the unity of the Spirit in the bond
of peace.
The peace of the Lord be always with you
and also with you.

THE BLESSING

God's grace go with you,
Christ's goodness be about you,
the Spirit's guidance lead you,
that you may walk in the way of peace;
and the blessing...

Proper 14

Sunday between 7 and 13 August inclusive

———

Track 1
2 Samuel 18. 5–9, 15, 31–33
Ps. 130
Ephesians 4.25—5.2
John 6. 35, 41–51

Track 2
1 Kings 19. 4–8
Ps. 34. 1–8
Ephesians 4.25—5.2
John 6. 35, 41–51

Lord Jesus, true bread from heaven, giving life and refreshment
to the world, fill our lives with your goodness, fill your church
with your presence, that we may live and work to your praise
and glory, who, with the Father and the Holy Spirit, are one
God, now and for ever. **Amen.**

Lord God, giver of all good gifts, we thank you for all that
    satisfies and sustains us,
for all the love you have given to us.
We pray for the right use of talents within your church,
that gifts and possessions may be neither hoarded nor
    squandered;
that the young may be given a good example to follow.
Lord, make us a gracious people, a generous people.
Lord our God,
you are our hope and our strength.

We give thanks for all who labour to provide for us;
we pray for any whose work is hard or tedious.
Guide all who influence the well-being of the earth.
We pray for workers in industries, factories or mines;

for ecologists and all who work in conservation,
for the protection of the rain forests.
Lord our God,
you are our hope and our strength.

Lord of all beauty, we pray for areas defaced or destroyed;
we remember people in wretched dwellings and slums,
all who are in areas deprived of beauty, or whose lives are in
    danger.
Lord, be with us in our homes and with our loved ones.
Lord our God,
you are our hope and our strength.

Father, the protector of all, we pray for any deprived of work,
of their homes, of their well-being;
We remember all whose land has been ravaged by war,
all places that have been pillaged through greed.
We pray for all whose harvests will fail this year.
We remember also all who have become ill,
    especially ....
Lord our God,
you are our hope and our strength.

Glory to you, Lord, for all who have passed beyond hunger and
thirst and have tasted of heavenly food, all who rejoice in life
everlasting. We pray for friends and loved ones who have gone
before us.
Lord our God,
you are our hope and our strength.

THE PEACE

Be kind to one another, tender-hearted to one another,
forgiving one another, as Christ has forgiven us.
The peace of the Lord be always with you
and also with you.

Live in love, as Christ loved us and gave himself for us;
let us give ourselves for each other's good;
and the blessing...

Proper 15

Sunday between 14 and 20 August inclusive

———

Track 1	Track 2
1 Kings 2. 10–12; 3. 3–14	Proverbs 9. 1–6
Ps. 111	Ps. 34. 9–14
Ephesians 5. 15–20	Ephesians 5. 15–20
John 6. 51–58	John 6. 51–58

Father, we give you thanks for all that you have done for us,
for life and the love that you bestow upon us.
Lord make us mindful of your gifts, that we may be content and
    grateful,
giving our love and lives to you all our days;
through Jesus Christ our Lord, who lives and reigns with you,
one God for ever. **Amen.**

Heavenly Father, you have shown us the way of life,
help us to walk in your ways and to do your will.
We pray for all who are dedicating their lives to you;
for the newly baptized and recently confirmed,
for all who are seeking and enquiring about their faith.
Guide all prayer groups and Bible studies.
We pray for hymn-writers, musicians and choirs.

Lord, may we sing your praises
and make music in our hearts to you.

Direct all who beautify our world by their talents,
all who improve our world by their actions.
We pray for artists, architects and planners,
for park-keepers and gardeners, all horticulturalists.
Bless all actors, singers and dancers, all entertainers.
Lord, may we sing your praises
and make music in our hearts to you.

We give you thanks for the gifts you have given to us.
We pray for a sharing of talents in our communities,
for your blessing on all councillors and group leaders.
Bless our homes and loved ones with your joy and peace.
Lord, may we sing your praises
and make music in our hearts to you.

Lord, bring light to all who live in darkness and hatred.
We pray for all caught up in bitterness or evil thoughts,
all who are tempted to do criminal acts or lead others astray.
We pray for all who are in sickness or in trouble,
for all who mourn and all who are sad.
Lord, may we sing your praises
and make music in our hearts to you.

We rejoice with all who praise you in the glory of your
    kingdom,
we sing your praises with angels and archangels and all the
    company of heaven.
We pray for loved ones departed.
Lord, may we sing your praises
and make music in our hearts to you.

Rejoice in the Lord: sing and make melody in your hearts to
your God.
The peace of the Lord be always with you
and also with you.

THE BLESSING

The joy of the creating Father be your strength.
The love of the ascended Saviour uplift your spirit.
The power of the Holy Spirit sustain you.
And the blessing...

Proper 16

Sunday between 21 and 27 August inclusive

Track 1
1 Kings 8. [1, 6, 10–11], 22–30, 41–43
Ps. 84
Ephesians 6. 10–20
John 6. 56–69

Track 2
Joshua 24. 1–2a, 14–18
Ps. 34. 15–22
Ephesians 6. 10–20
John 6. 56–69

Mighty God, in you is our hope and our strength,
you are a very present help in all our troubles.
Grant that putting on the whole armour of God
we may be able to stand against the powers of darkness
and proclaim your saving gospel of love and peace;
through Jesus Christ our Lord,

who lives and reigns with you and the Holy Spirit,
one God for ever. **Amen.**

Holy God, Holy and Strong One, Holy and Mighty One,
all power, all might, all energy and all strength comes from you;
equip us to stand against the evils of our time:
give us the shield of faith, the sword of the spirit, the helmet of
   salvation, the girdle of truth, the breastplate of righteousness
   and protect us with the gospel of peace, that we may remain
   loyal to the end.
Strengthen all who are working in places of degradation,
all who are facing danger, violence and oppression.
Lord, you are our hope.
Our strength is in you.

Lord, guide all who are powerful leaders in our world,
all rulers, statespersons and politicians.
We pray for all who have power at work as managers, shop
   stewards and union leaders.
We remember all who feel powerless, all driven by economic
   forces.
Lord, you are our hope.
Our strength is in you.

We praise you for all who have revealed your power and
   presence to us.
We pray for all teachers: may they encourage a sense of awe and
   wonder.
We remember especially nursery schools and primary schools.
We ask your blessing on our homes and loved ones.
Lord, you are our hope.
Our strength is in you.

Healing God, be with the broken-hearted and all whose spirits
   are crushed.
Bless all who are facing difficult times ahead,
all who are struggling to survive, all who are fearful and anxious.

We pray for all who are in sickness,
especially ....
Lord, you are our hope.
Our strength is in you.

We rejoice with those who have triumphed, with all in your
nearer presence.
We join with all who have found their strength in you.
We pray for loved ones who are in your glorious kingdom.
Lord, you are our hope.
Our strength is in you.

THE PEACE

Find your strength and your peace in the Lord and in his mighty
power.
The peace of the Lord be always with you
and also with you.

THE BLESSING

God, the Mighty One, defend you on every side.
Christ, the Redeemer, deliver you from all evil.
The Spirit of God strengthen you in all goodness.
And the blessing...

Proper 17

Sunday between 28 August and 3 September inclusive

Track 1
Song of Solomon 2. 8–13
Ps. 45. 1–2, 6–7 (*or* 1–7)
James 1. 17–27
Mark 7. 1–8, 14–15, 21–23

Track 2
Deuteronomy 4. 1–2, 6–9
Ps. 15
James 1. 17–27
Mark 7. 1–8, 14–15, 21–23

Make clean our hearts, O God, and renew a right spirit within
us, that we may seek to serve you in joy and gladness and bring
others into the glory of your love; through Jesus Christ our
Lord, who is alive and reigns with you and the Holy Spirit, one
God for ever. **Amen.**

Holy God, make us holy; give us power to resist evil,
give us strength to do what is right.
Lord, make us a generous people, a hospitable people.
We pray for the church working in areas of hatred,
where Christians are facing hostility and violence,
where to become a Christian is to risk loss and rejection.
Holy and Strong One,
hear our prayer.

Protect, O Lord, all who are working for liberty and freedom,
all who are risking their lives for justice and peace.
We pray for all peace-makers and peace-keepers,
for all who seek to reconcile divided communities or peoples.
Holy and Strong One,
hear our prayer.

God of love, we pray for all homes where love has grown cold,
for all people where life has become dull routine,
for all who are bored or tired of life,
for all betrayed by a loved one or a friend;
Lord, that we may never take anyone for granted,
that we may not misuse the power and freedom we have.
Holy and Strong One,
hear our prayer.

We pray for all who have become bankrupt or are in great debt;
we remember the world's poor, all being treated with contempt,
all who have nothing to call their own.
We pray for all who have suffered from a heart attack or stroke,
all who are on a life-support machine,
all who are struggling to survive.
Holy and Strong One,
hear our prayer.

Bless our loved ones departed who are renewed and restored to
the fullness of life and are inheritors with the saints in light;
may we share with them in the glory that is to come.
Holy and Strong One,
hear our prayer.

THE PEACE

Seek for peace:
peace in your heart, peace in your spirit,
peace in your mind, peace in your home.
The peace of the Lord be always with you
and also with you.

THE BLESSING

The Lord lead you from hostility to hospitality, from darkness
to light: the Lord renew and refresh you; and the blessing...

Proper 18

Sunday between 4 and 10 September inclusive

Lord, open our lives to your goodness.
Open our eyes to your presence.
Open our ears to your call.
Open our hearts to your love.
Open our lips to your praises.
Open us to your glory. **Amen.**

We give you thanks and praise for your life-giving and
life-extending love.
May your church help others to extend their lives and to rejoice
in your world.
We pray for all who are working for justice and freedom of
captives,
for all who seek to bring food to the hungry and comfort to the
lonely.
Lord, as you raise us up, help us to lift others out of their
troubles.
Our God is here.
He comes to save us.

We remember all who have worked hard and achieved nothing,
all who have laboured in vain, all whose work has been
   frustrating,
all whose work or livelihood has been destroyed.
We pray for the unemployed, the homeless, all who hunger and
   thirst.
Our God is here.
He comes to save us.

God, strengthen the bonds of community where we live;
direct all who have dealings with groups or the care of
   individuals.
We pray for all who feel isolated or cut off from others.
We pray for our own homes and loved ones.
Our God is here.
He comes to save us.

We pray for all who have difficulty in communicating with
   others,
those with hearing and speech difficulties, and the blind.
We remember all who are mentally or severely physically
   handicapped.
We pray for those caring for children with autism or adults with
   learning difficulties.
For all who are finding their lives restricted through illness.
Our God is here.
He comes to save us.

Blessed are you, Lord our God, you have opened for us the
   kingdom of heaven.
We remember before you the whole company of saints, and
   pray for our loved ones departed.
Our God is here.
He comes to save us.

As much as is possible, live in peace,
share peace, pray for peace.
The peace of the Lord be always with you
and also with you.

The Lord touch your heart with his love and open your life to
his glory; and the blessing...

Proper 19

Sunday between 11 and 17 September inclusive

———

Track 1
Proverbs 1. 20–33
Ps. 19. 1–6 [7–14] *or Canticle*:
Wisdom of Solomon 7.26—8.1
James 3. 1–12
Mark 8. 27–38

Track 2
Isaiah 50. 4–9a
Ps. 116. 1–9
James 3. 1–12
Mark 8. 27–38

O Lord, as Peter confessed you as the Christ, give us boldness to
proclaim your redeeming love and saving power in the world;
may we be ready to bear the cross and give ourselves for others
and the advancement of your kingdom; we ask this in your
Name, Jesus our Lord, who with the Father and the Holy Spirit
are one God, now and for ever. **Amen.**

Fill, O Lord, your church with wisdom, that it may reflect your love and light and be an image of your goodness. Lord, may we confess Jesus as our Christ and Saviour, not only in word but by the way we live, and so bring others to a deeper awareness of your love.

Guide all who preach and teach in your Name.
We pray for a deepening of unity among all Christians.
Father, hear us,
in the Name of Christ our Lord.

Bless with your wisdom all places of learning.
We pray for schools, colleges and training establishments:
for all lecturers, teachers and trainers of people.
We pray for all who influence our minds through broadcasting or the press,
for all involved in publishing and printing.
Father, hear us,
in the Name of Christ our Lord.

We give thanks for those who gave us confidence to venture and to risk,
all who have given us strength to stand on our own feet.
We pray for all who lack confidence, all who have a low esteem of themselves.
We give thanks for and pray for our homes and our neighbours.
Father, hear us,
in the Name of Christ our Lord.

Lord, support all who are fearful and anxious,
all who are timid and afraid to venture.
We pray for all who doubt their own ability or your love.
We remember all who are lonely or desperate;
we pray for the suicidal.
We remember also all who are in pain or distress.
Father, hear us,
in the Name of Christ our Lord.

We give you praise with your saints in glory,
all who have confessed the faith and are in your kingdom.
We pray for all who are departed from this life,
 especially ....
Father, hear us,
in the Name of Christ our Lord.

THE PEACE

Christ is our life. Christ is our Saviour. Christ is our hope.
Christ is our peace.
The peace of the Lord be always with you
and also with you.

THE BLESSING

God give you grace to confess the faith of Christ crucified.
God give you strength to offer yourself to him;
and the blessing...

Proper 20

Sunday between 18 and 24 September inclusive

———

Track 1
Proverbs 31. 10–31
Ps. 1
James 3.13—4.3, 7–8a
Mark 9. 30–37

Track 2
Wisdom of Solomon 1.16—2.1, 12–22 *or*
Jeremiah 11. 18–20
Ps. 54
James 3.13—4.3, 7–8a
Mark 9. 30–37

Holy Father, give us a spirit of contentment and peace, that we
 may enjoy who we are and what we have.
Help us not only to appreciate what you have given us, but to
 be gracious and generous to others.
May the world's goods be neither hoarded nor squandered but
 used for the benefit of all;
through Jesus Christ our Lord, who with you and the Holy
 Spirit are One God, for ever. **Amen.**

We give you thanks for your peace in our hearts and minds,
that deep peace which comes from you alone.
Make your church an instrument of peace, of love and healing.
We pray for areas of conflict within the church.
O God, by your power,
defend us and give your peace.

Bring your gift of peace to places of war and unrest,
to peoples being destroyed by greed and selfishness.
We pray for all people who are abused by the ambition of
 others.

We remember all who are never content or satisfied,
and all who find no rest unless they rest in you and your love.
O God, by your power,
defend us and give your peace.

God, grant your grace to the communities to which we belong,
that there may be good communication between peoples.
We pray for public officials and all who deliver to our homes.
Give your peace in our homes, in our work and in all our
    dealings.
O God, by your power,
defend us and give your peace.

Comfort, O Lord, all who have been betrayed or deserted,
all who have been misunderstood or persecuted.
We pray for hostages and prisoners of conscience.
We remember all who are lonely in their sickness,
we pray for all who are ill at home or in hospital.
O God, by your power,
defend us and give your peace.

We give you thanks for the victory of our Lord Jesus Christ
    over death, and for the gift of eternal life. We pray for friends
    and loved ones who are with you in glory.
O God, by your power,
defend us and give your peace.

THE PEACE

A harvest of righteousness is sown in peace for those who make
peace and spread it abroad.
The peace of the Lord be always with you
and also with you.

Draw near to God and his love, and he will draw near to you.
Resist the devil and all his works, and he will flee from you.
And the blessing...

Proper 21

Sunday between 25 September and 1 October inclusive

———

Track 1
Esther 7. 1–6, 9–10; 9. 20–22
Ps. 124
James 5. 13–20
Mark 9. 38–50

Track 2
Numbers 11. 4–6, 10–16, 24–29
Ps. 19. 7–14
James 5. 13–20
Mark 9. 38–50

Lord our God,
on the way of goodness, if we stumble lift us up;
on the way of holiness, if we stray bring us back;
on the way of kindness, if we toughen soften our hearts;
that we may draw others to you and your saving power,
by our words and our example;
through Jesus Christ our Lord,
who with you and the Holy Spirit are one God for ever and
    ever. **Amen.**

Strengthen, O Lord, your church in its care for the needy.
We pray for all healers and healing communities,
for those who practise the laying on of hands,
for spiritual guides and counsellors.
We remember all who come for forgiveness, hope and comfort;

we commit ourselves to your saving power.
Our help is in the Name of the Lord,
the Maker of heaven and earth.

We pray for all who are seeking to reclaim and restore spoiled
areas.
Give hope to all who live in slums and poor housing,
all whose land is exhausted and whose labour is frustrated.
Bless all who are caring for and seeking to re-house refugees.
We pray for all who are seeking political asylum.
Our help is in the Name of the Lord,
the Maker of heaven and earth.

Lord, teach us to be open and generous in our dealings.
May we dedicate ourselves to the service of others and to you.
Bless the neighbourhood in which we live and the place where
we work.
We pray for our friends and our families.
Our help is in the Name of the Lord,
the Maker of heaven and earth.

Lord of all power, support all whose strength is gone,
the totally exhausted, the world-weary, all who feel dried up;
we think of those who cannot cope on their own.
We remember also all who suffer from malnutrition, from
hunger and thirst.
Our help is in the Name of the Lord,
the Maker of heaven and earth.

We give you praise for the victory that is ours in Christ Jesus,
for the promise of joy and peace in your eternal kingdom.
We pray that our loved ones departed may be numbered with
your saints in glory.
Our help is in the Name of the Lord,
the Maker of heaven and earth.

THE PEACE

Accept the peace that God gives, share that peace with others.
Live in peace, the peace that only God can give.
The peace of the Lord be always with you
and also with you.

THE BLESSING

To the Mighty God, who is able to keep you from falling,
to the Saving Christ, who upholds all that are down,
to the powerful Spirit who restores us to life,
to our loving and life-giving God be glory and praise;
and the blessing...

Proper 22

Sunday between 2 and 8 October inclusive

———

Track 1
Job 1. 1; 2. 1–10
Ps. 26
Hebrews 1. 1–4; 2. 5–12
Mark 10. 2–16

Track 2
Genesis 2. 18–24
Ps. 8
Hebrews 1. 1–4; 2. 5–12
Mark 10. 2–16

Good and gracious God, your love is never-failing,
your heart is open to us, your presence never leaves us;
strengthen our faith, deepen our love for you and keep us in
    your ways;
through Jesus Christ our Lord,

who lives and reigns with you and the Holy Spirit,
one God, for ever. **Amen.**

Holy Father, bless your church, that it may reveal your love:
let us be an open and accepting church;
let us be a forgiving and a sensitive church;
let us be a loving and an understanding church;
that your church may reflect your love for the world.
Lord, our Redeemer,
have mercy upon us.

Lord, comfort all who are having any difficulties in their
relationships.
We pray for all who find it hard to make friends,
for all who have been betrayed or deserted by a loved one.
We remember all who have to face violence in their homes or at
work.
We pray for all who cannot trust the people around them.
Lord, our Redeemer,
have mercy upon us.

Lord, in our dealings with each other,
teach us to listen, teach us to forgive,
teach us to understand, teach us to love,
give us the courage to start again.
We pray for our friends and loved ones.
Lord, our Redeemer,
have mercy upon us.

God of love, give strength to all from broken homes:
we pray for any where there is little love or understanding,
for all families that are needing help and attention.
We pray for all who are separated from loved ones through
sickness,
for all who are lonely and live alone.
Lord, our Redeemer,
have mercy upon us.

Praise to you, O God, for in Christ Jesus so many are brought
   into love and glory.
We give thanks for your saints dwelling in everlasting light.
We pray for loved ones departed,
   especially for ....
Lord, our Redeemer,
have mercy upon us.

THE PEACE

Jesus is not ashamed to call us his brothers and sisters;
today he enfolds us in his love and peace.
The peace of the Lord be always with you
and also with you.

THE BLESSING

The love of the Creator be all around you,
the love of the Saviour be above and beneath you,
the love of the Holy Spirit be within you;
and the blessing . . .

Proper 23

Sunday between 9 and 15 October inclusive

———

Track 1
Job 23. 1–9, 16–17
Ps. 22. 1–15
Hebrews 4. 12–16
Mark 10. 17–31

Track 2
Amos 5. 6–7, 10–15
Ps. 90. 12–17
Hebrews 4. 12–16
Mark 10. 17–31

Holy and Strong One, we praise you for Jesus Christ our great
High Priest, who has entered into the fullness of the kingdom in
heaven and opened for us the gate of glory. May we approach
the throne of grace with boldness, and in the time of need know
your mercy and grace; through Christ our King, who lives and
reigns with you and the Holy Spirit, one God, for ever. **Amen.**

Lord, we pray that we may seek you and so enter into life.
We pray for all who seek you in simplicity and humility,
for all who find you in their service of others.
Bless all who are in religious communities, and all seeking to
    consecrate their lives to you.
We pray for any who have lost their faith or their way.
Lord, give us grace
and help in all our needs.

We pray for all who are choked by their riches,
for people possessed by their possessions,
for all who are afraid to give and afraid to share,
for all who have amassed wealth but are poor in spirit,
for all who are suffering through the greed and avarice of others.

Lord, give us grace
and help in all our needs.

God, we thank you for all who have sacrificed for us,
for all who have enriched our lives by their goodness,
for all who have been gracious and generous to us.
Teach us to be generous and willing to give.
We pray for our friends and families.
Lord, give us grace
and help in all our needs.

We pray for all who are over-worked and the work-weary,
for all who lack freedom and suffer through injustice,
for all who are denied basic human needs.
We pray for all who are ill or are in need of help.
Lord, give us grace
and help in all our needs.

We give thanks for all who have entered into glory,
for all who have triumphed over darkness and evil.
We pray for loved ones departed.
Lord, give us grace
and help in all our needs.

THE PEACE

As we have a great High Priest who has passed into the heavens,
let us approach the throne of grace with boldness.
The peace of the Lord be always with you
and also with you.

THE BLESSING

God our heavenly Father, whose Son, our Lord Jesus Christ,
took the form of a servant, grant that you may serve him
through serving others; and the blessing...

Proper 24

Sunday between 16 and 22 October inclusive

Christ, our great High Priest, you deal gently with the ignorant and the wayward; in your great goodness lead us into the ways of justice and peace, that we may faithfully serve you on earth until we rejoice in your kingdom in glory. **Amen.**

Lord, as you have called us, make us worthy of our calling.
Let us see you in others: let others see you in us.
Make us more sensitive to others and their needs,
make us more ready to help and to show our care.
Lord, make us a serving church, a giving church, a loving
    church.
Lord in heaven,
hear us and help us.

We pray for the world's poor, for desert-dwellers and places
    where crops have failed,
for all who have suffered from floods or other disasters,
for all who have no place to call home,
for street children and displaced persons.
Lord in heaven,
hear us and help us.

Lord, make us useful in the community in which we live.
Make us gracious, make us generous,
make us aware of where we can help.
We pray for loved ones and friends, especially any in need.
Lord in heaven,
hear us and help us.

Lord, be a strength to all who are finding life difficult,
for any with difficult decisions to make,
any having difficulty at work or in their relationships.
We pray for those who await operations or the doctor's
    diagnosis,
for all sitting by the bed of a loved one who is ill,
for all suffering peoples.
Lord in heaven,
hear us and help us.

THE PEACE

God's grace and goodness go with you and give you his peace.
The peace of the Lord be always with you
and also with you.

THE BLESSING

God, who has called you into life and to love him, make you
worthy of your calling; strengthen, establish, settle you; and the
blessing...

Proper 25

Sunday between 23 and 29 October inclusive

———

Track 1
Job 42. 1–6, 10–17
Ps. 34. 1–8 [19–22]
Hebrews 7. 23–28
Mark 10. 46–52

Track 2
Jeremiah 31. 7–9
Ps. 126
Hebrews 7. 23–28
Mark 10. 46–52

Lord, open our eyes to your presence.
Grant us a vision to see what we can achieve:
as your love touches us may we reach out to others.
Lord, stretch our capabilities, extend our vision and increase
our sense of purpose, that we may grow in our service of you;
through Jesus Christ our Lord, who with you, in the unity of
the Holy Spirit, are one God for ever. **Amen.**

We praise you for all men and women of vision,
for all who through their insight have built up your church and
    world.
We pray for writers, musicians and craftspeople,
for church synods and councils,
for our bishop and all who minister to us.
Lord, open our eyes,
that we may behold your glory.

Bless, O Lord, all who are inventors and research workers,
all who seek to improve and enhance our world,
all planners, builders and manufacturers;

Lord, grant to each insight into what effect they are having on the world.
Lord, open our eyes,
that we may behold your glory.

We thank you for all who through their goodness have provided for us,
all who provided for our schooling and our care.
We pray for the National Health Service,
for doctors, dentists and nurses.
We pray for all our friends and loved ones.
Lord, open our eyes,
that we may behold your glory.

We pray for all who have lost vision, all for whom the future looks bleak,
all who have lost their way, all who through lack of insight are in trouble.
We pray for all whose sight is impaired and all who are blind,
for all who write in Braille, and for the Royal Commonwealth Society for the Blind.
Lord, open our eyes,
that we may behold your glory.

We give thanks for all whose vision is now lost in clear sight,
all who behold your glory. We pray for loved ones departed.
Lord, open our eyes,
that we may behold your glory.

THE PEACE

Come, taste and see that the Lord is good; happy are they that trust in him.
The peace of the Lord be always with you
and also with you.

The Lord reveal to you the hidden glory of his presence,
open your eyes to behold that he is ever with you:
and the blessing...

Bible Sunday

Isaiah 55. 1–11 : Ps. 19. 7–14 : 2 Timothy 3.14—4.5 : John 5. 36b–47

Father, we give you thanks for your holy word spoken of old by
the prophets and apostles, for all that is written in the
Scriptures, that is proclaimed by evangelists and preachers;
we pray that we may heed your word and come to know the
Word made flesh, even Jesus Christ our Lord, who lives and
reigns with you and the Holy Spirit, one God for ever. **Amen.**

We thank you for the word that has been a lantern to our feet
and a light to our path,
for all the guidance and hope we get through the Scriptures.
Bless your church as it seeks to proclaim your word for today;
we pray for all theologians, preachers and teachers.
Above all, may we come to know the true and living Word,
Jesus Christ our Lord.
We remember all who have never heard the Good News or not
accepted it.
Let your word come forth
and give us light.

God, direct all who are seeking to live an upright life,
all who are seeking guidance, all who are wanting to do what is
right.
We pray that our leaders may be people of honesty and integrity,
that they may be compassionate in their dealings and seek
righteousness.
Give wisdom to all who influence our minds and our hearts.
Let your word come forth
and give us light.

We give thanks for tradition, and for those who have handed on
to us the wisdom of the past.
Bless all who have looked into the past as a guide to the present;
we pray especially for Bible students and Bible study groups.
We pray for our loved ones and all with whom we share our faith,
that we may live by and proclaim your holy word.
Let your word come forth
and give us light.

We pray for all anxious people who lack a word of comfort or
of hope;
all who are at war with themselves or others, that they may
hear your word of peace;
all who are lonely and feel forsaken, that they may know the
Word made flesh.
We pray for hospital chaplains and for all who bring hope to
the troubled.
Let your word come forth
and give us light.

Blessed are all who have heard the word of God and kept it to
the end.
We give thanks for the Apostles and Evangelists with all your
saints;
we pray for our loved ones departed.
Let your word come forth
and give us light.

Let the Word of God dwell in your heart and keep you in peace.
The peace of the Lord be always with you
and also with you.

THE BLESSING

In the presence of God, and of the Lord Jesus who is the Word
made flesh, proclaim the message in the power of the Spirit with
the utmost patience, in teaching and by example: and the
blessing...

Dedication Festival

The First Sunday in October or Last Sunday after Trinity

———

Genesis 28. 11–18 *or* Revelation 21. 9–14 : Ps. 122 : 1 Peter 2. 1–10 :
John 10. 22–29

Lord, through your holy church you come to us,
you give us yourself, you give us your love;
may we dedicate our love, ourselves to you,
Lord of the church, Father, Son and Holy Spirit. **Amen.**

Bless, O Lord, this church, which has sought to worship you;
Lord, make us holy as you are holy, that we may be a dedicated
    people.
We give thanks for Saint .... in whose name
    our church is dedicated;

may we follow *his/her* example of love and service.
We pray for all who have worshipped here since the church was
  founded,
all who have been baptized, confirmed, married or buried from
  this church,
all who have found strength and hope, peace and forgiveness
  through this place.
Lord of the church,
you are our Lord and our God.

We give thanks for all who live dedicated lives in our world,
all who by sacrifice and goodness maintain the fabric of our
  society.
We pray for all who are quietly giving their lives in the service
  of others,
for all who are caring for neighbours or the needy,
For all who in the Name of God are reaching out in love.
Lord of the church,
you are our Lord and our God.

Today (in this church) we dedicate ourselves to you,
we give you our joys and our sorrows,
our success and our failures, our strength and our weakness.
Take us, Lord, use us in the service of others,
and for the furtherance of your kingdom.
Lord of the church,
you are our Lord and our God.

We pray for all who are the church but cannot come to church,
all who are hindered through disability or weakness,
all who are prevented by old age or infirmity.
We pray especially for .... and thank you for
  all they have done for church and community.
Lord of the church,
you are our Lord and our God.

Blessed are all who have served you faithfully through the years and have been an example to us. We pray for all who have led and sustained the worship of this church and now worship you with the saints in glory.
Lord of the church,
you are our Lord and our God.

THE PEACE

The Lord is in this place, his presence fills it, his presence is peace.
The peace of the Lord be always with you
and also with you.

THE BLESSING

God gives himself this day to you, give yourself to God.
Go out dedicated to him and live and work to his glory;
and the blessing...

All Saints' Day

Sunday between 30 October and 5 November or, if this is not kept as All Saints' Sunday, on 1 November itself

Wisdom 3. 1–9 *or* Isaiah 25. 6–9 : Ps. 24. 1–6 : Revelation 21. 1–6a : John 11. 32–44

Holy Lord, take us and make us holy,
make us yours and make us obedient,
make us faithful, make us joyful and

make us to be numbered with your saints,
in that glory which is everlasting;
through Jesus Christ our Lord, who is alive and reigns with
    you,
in the unity of the Holy Spirit, one God for ever. **Amen.**

We join our praises with all who have kept the faith,
all who have been loyal and true,
all who have served and witnessed,
all who have been holy and examples to us.
Lord, make your church a holy church, a praying church, a
    giving church, a serving church.
We give thanks for the saints who have inspired us, may we be
    an inspiration to others.
Holy God,
make us holy.

We remember all who have sacrificed and laid down their lives
    for others.
We pray for all who are seeking to live in simplicity,
all who are leading dedicated lives,
all who are giving themselves on behalf of others,
all who give their time and talents in the service of humankind.
Holy God,
make us holy.

We give thanks for all who have led us into the ways of
    holiness,
for all who have shared their vision, and their love.
We pray for all schools, colleges and universities.
Bless, O Lord, our homes, that they may reveal your love.
Holy God,
make us holy.

We pray for all who are living heroic lives amidst troubles;
Lord, that the weak may know your strength,
that the troubled may know your peace,

that the fearful may know your love,
that the lonely may know your presence.
Lord, may all who are in need know that you protect them and
enfold them in your love.
Holy God,
make us holy.

We rejoice in the fellowship of all your saints, with all the
faithful departed,
and commend to you our friends and loved ones who have
departed from us.
Holy God,
make us holy.

THE PEACE

God give you the peace of the blessed, the peace that the world
cannot give,
the peace that passes all understanding.
The peace of the Lord be always with you
and also with you.

THE BLESSING

The Lord give you his grace and make you to be numbered with
his saints in that glory which is everlasting; and the blessing . . .

Sundays Before Advent

The Fourth Sunday Before Advent

*Sunday between 30 October and 5 November inclusive. For use if the
Feast of All Saints was celebrated on 1 November and alternative
propers are needed.*

———

Deuteronomy 6. 1–9 : Ps. 119. 1–8 : Hebrews 9. 11–14 : Mark 12. 28–34

Lord, we give our lives to you,
our mind and all its thinking,
our heart and all its loving,
our strength and all its working,
our soul and all its worshipping:
we give ourselves to you,
and seek to serve you in our neighbour;
through Jesus Christ our Lord,
who lives with you and the Holy Spirit,
one God for ever and ever. **Amen.**

Lord, let it be seen that we have been with you,
let there be traces of glory in our lives.
Fill with your radiance all who lead worship,
all who preach, all who reach out in mission.
We remember all who, in your Name, care for the outcasts and
  the needy in our world.

We ask your blessing on all relief organizations.
You are our shelter, O God.
Lord, keep us in all troubles.

We give thanks for all who serve others in their work.
We pray for workers in industry, in shops and hotels.
We remember those who clean our streets,
and those concerned with the well-being of the earth.
We pray for social workers and for the Samaritans,
for all who seek to be good neighbours;
and for the neighbourhood to which we belong.
You are our shelter, O God.
Lord, keep us in all troubles.

We give thanks for all who have been a support or a guide to us.
We pray for any in our neighbourhood who are lonely,
for all who feel neglected or rejected.
We give you thanks for our homes and our loved ones.
You are our shelter, O God.
Lord, keep us in all troubles.

Lord, be a strength to all who have suffered through the greed,
    the insensitivity, or the violence of others.
We remember areas where the land has been spoiled and people
    hunger.
We pray for those who have been driven out of their land and
    homes.
Lord, bless all who are in illness or in pain,
    especially ....
You are our shelter, O God.
Lord, keep us in all troubles.

Lord, you welcome into your kingdom all who have searched
    for you,
and all who have served you:
we pray for friends and loved ones departed.
You are our shelter, O God.
Lord, keep us in all troubles.

The peace of God the Creator,
the peace of Christ the Redeemer,
the peace of the Spirit the Sanctifier,
The peace of the One, the peace of the Three;
the peace of the Lord be always with you
and also with you.

The power and peace of the presence protect you and keep you
from all harm; and the blessing...

The Third Sunday Before Advent

Sunday between 6 and 12 November inclusive

———

Jonah 3. 1–5, 10 : Ps. 62. 5–12 : Hebrews 9. 24–28 : Mark 1. 14–20

Lord, you have called us to know you,
you have called us to love you,
you have called us to serve you,
you have called us to proclaim you:
guide and strengthen us by your Spirit,
make us worthy of our calling,
that we may live to your praise and glory;
through Jesus Christ our Lord,
who is alive and reigns with you and the same Spirit,
one God for ever. **Amen.**

Holy Father, strengthen each in their vocation and ministry:
help us to see how we need each other,
and to share the talents and abilities which you give to us.
Guide by your Holy Spirit all who are called to ordination:
we pray for theological colleges, for tutors and students,
for all who are seeking to serve others.
Lord, as you have called us,
make us worthy of our calling.

Grant grace to all who care for others in their daily work;
we pray for doctors, nurses and ambulance workers,
for the fire brigade and the police and social workers.
We remember also shopkeepers and bakers;
Lord, that each of them may show love and care in their actions.
Lord, as you have called us,
make us worthy of our calling.

We give you thanks and praise for all who have cared for us.
Bless with your goodness our homes and loved ones.
Strengthen us in the service of our community.
Guide us that we may bring joy and peace to others.
Lord, as you have called us,
make us worthy of our calling.

Holy and Strong One,
be a comfort to all who have been hindered in living their lives
    to the full.
We remember all whose vocation has been thwarted through
    illness,
through poverty, through the prejudice of others.
We pray for all who are unemployed or have been made
    redundant,
for all who feel their lives are being wasted.
We pray for all in sickness or weakness,
    especially ....
Lord, as you have called us,
make us worthy of our calling.

We give you praise for all who have fulfilled their work on earth
and now serve before you in your glorious kingdom.
We pray for our loved ones departed,
    especially ....
May we at the last rejoice with them in life everlasting.
Lord, as you have called us,
make us worthy of our calling.

THE PEACE

God is ever close at hand, his kingdom is near;
come and enter into his love and peace.
The peace of the Lord be always with you
and also with you.

THE BLESSING

The God of grace who has called us to his eternal glory in
Christ Jesus, make you perfect; establish, strengthen, settle you:
and the blessing . . .

The Second Sunday Before Advent

Sunday between 13 and 19 November inclusive

Daniel 12. 1–3 : Ps. 16 : Hebrews 10. 11–14 [15–18] 19–25 : Mark 13. 1–8

God of all power and might, give us grace to trust you in the
darkness as well as in the light. In the face of danger and
adversity be our strength and hope, that we may live and work

146

to your praise and glory; through Jesus Christ our Lord, who is alive and reigns with you and the Holy Spirit, one God for ever. **Amen.**

God, the strength of all that trust in you, without whom
    nothing is strong,
give us courage to stand for the truth,
courage to proclaim the gospel,
courage to persevere in times of trouble.
Give us a mind to know what is good and true.
Give us a will to be faithful to you.
Give us a heart to love and serve you.
We pray for Christians working in dangerous places,
for all who are facing persecution for their faith,
for all who suffer mockery and scorn.
God is our strength and salvation.
In him we will not be afraid.

God of love, may we learn to live in harmony and peace.
We pray for all places where there is war or rumour of war,
where there is violence, oppression, or tyranny;
for all places of unrest, crime or neglect.
Strengthen all who work for freedom and justice.
God is our strength and salvation.
In him we will not be afraid.

We pray for the place where we work,
and we remember all that are over-worked or discriminated
    against.
We pray for any without a proper wage or a dependable
    income.
We give thanks for our homes and our loved ones.
God is our strength and salvation.
In him we will not be afraid.

Lord of all, give hope and strength to all caught up in disasters,
all who are suffering from famine or flood,

all caught up in storms or earthquakes.
Give courage to all who have fallen ill,
all whose sickness finds no cure,
all who are afraid for their future.
God is our strength and salvation.
In him we will not be afraid.

We give thanks for those who are now where sorrow and pain
 are no more:
we rejoice in the fellowship of your saints,
and commend our loved ones departed to your almighty love.
God is our strength and salvation.
In him we will not be afraid.

THE PEACE

Strive for peace, live in peace, share your peace.
The peace of the Lord be always with you
and also with you.

THE BLESSING

Abide in the presence of the Almighty, let your life be filled with
traces of his glory; and the blessing...

Christist the King

Sunday between 20 and 26 November inclusive

Daniel 7. 9–10, 13–14 : Ps. 93 : Revelation 1. 4b–8 : John 18. 33–37

You are the King of Glory, O Christ, you are the everlasting
  Son of the Father.
We give you our love and offer you our lives.
Come, Lord, and rule in our hearts, until your kingdom come
  on earth as it is in heaven.
Come, Christ our King, and reign over us,
as you reign with the Father and the Holy Spirit one God for
  ever. **Amen.**

Christ, our King, keep us calm and faithful in all troubles;
let us not be afraid, for you rule over all and your kingdom will
  come.
Give strength and direction to all who seek to do your will,
to all who strive for peace, all who work for righteousness.
Guide all who proclaim your coming and your kingdom.
Lord, your kingdom come in us,
as it is in heaven.

Christ, our King, may we know you are ever present in all life,
you are there at the centre of power, where decisions are made;
yet you are with the weak and the humble whom no one notices.
We pray for all who seek justice and maintain order,
for all rulers and people in authority.
Lord, your kingdom come in us,
as it is in heaven.

Christ, our King, rule in our hearts and in our homes.
May love, peace and forgiveness be known among us;
may we seek to show we belong to you and you love us.
We pray for broken homes and broken-hearted people,
for all who have been deserted by loved ones.
Lord, your kingdom come in us,
as it is in heaven.

Christ, our King, give hope and vision to the suffering,
let them be aware of your love and your kingdom.
Keep, O Lord, in your grasp all who are losing their grip on life,
enfold in your love all who are fearful and anxious.
We pray for the troubled in body, mind or spirit;
we remember before you all who are ill.
Lord, your kingdom come in us,
as it is in heaven.

We give thanks that you are Lord of all, your kingdom cannot
     fail, death has no dominion over us.
We give thanks that your kingdom is an everlasting kingdom
     and our loved departed ones are with you in glory.
We pray for our friends and loved ones departed,
     especially ....
Lord, your kingdom come in us,
as it is in heaven.

THE PEACE

Grace to you and peace from God,
from him who is, who was and who is to come.
The peace of the Lord be always with you
and also with you.

THE BLESSING

To him who sits upon the throne, to the One true God, be praise and glory, for ever and ever; and the blessing...